TEACHER TIME MANAGEMENT

HOW TO **PRIORITIZE YOUR DAY**

SO YOU CAN **ENJOY YOUR EVENING**

ELLEN I. LINNI

Solution Tree | Press

Copyright © 2025 by Solution Tree Press

Materials appearing here are copyrighted. With one exception, all rights are reserved. Readers may reproduce only those pages marked "Reproducible." Otherwise, no part of this book may be reproduced or transmitted in any form or by any means (electronic, photocopying, recording, or otherwise) without prior written permission of the publisher.

AI output featured in the text generated with the assistance of OpenAI.

555 North Morton Street
Bloomington, IN 47404
800.733.6786 (toll free) / 812.336.7700
FAX: 812.336.7790

email: info@SolutionTree.com
SolutionTree.com

Visit **go.SolutionTree.com/teacherefficacy** to download the free reproducibles in this book.

Printed in the United States of America

Library of Congress Cataloging-in-Publication Data

Names: Linnihan, Ellen, author.
Title: Teacher time management : how to prioritize your day so you can enjoy your evening / Ellen I. Linnihan.
Description: Bloomington, IN : Solution Tree Press, 2025. | Includes bibliographical references and index.
Identifiers: LCCN 2024041407 (print) | LCCN 2024041408 (ebook) | ISBN 9781958590393 (paperback) | ISBN 9781958590409 (ebook)
Subjects: LCSH: Teachers--Workload | Teachers--Time management. | School day--Psychological aspects. | Work-life balance. | Teacher turnover--Prevention.
Classification: LCC LB2844.1.W6 L56 2025 (print) | LCC LB2844.1.W6 (ebook) | DDC 371.14/12--dc23/eng/20241008
LC record available at https://lccn.loc.gov/2024041407
LC ebook record available at https://lccn.loc.gov/2024041408

Solution Tree
Jeffrey C. Jones, CEO
Edmund M. Ackerman, President

Solution Tree Press
President and Publisher: Douglas M. Rife
Associate Publishers: Todd Brakke and Kendra Slayton
Editorial Director: Laurel Hecker
Art Director: Rian Anderson
Copy Chief: Jessi Finn
Senior Production Editor: Tonya Maddox Cupp
Text and Cover Designer: Fabiana Cochran
Proofreader: Elijah Oates
Acquisitions Editors: Carol Collins and Hilary Goff
Content Development Specialist: Amy Rubenstein
Associate Editors: Sarah Ludwig and Elijah Oates
Editorial Assistant: Madison Chartier

TABLE OF CONTENTS

Reproducibles are in italics.

About the Author vii

Introduction 1
    What a Mode Is 2
    Why This Book 3
    About This Book 5

Chapter 1: Your Goal and Streamlining 7
    Identify the Goal 8
    Let Students in on the Goal 9
    Determine Where You Can Streamline 10
    Streamline the Process 13
    Be Fluid 20
    Reflection Questions 21
        College Planning Sheet 22
        Preconference Form 23
        Peer Edit Rubric—Argument Research Paper 24
        Peer Analysis Form 26

iii

Chapter 2: Low Concentration Mode. 27
    Low Concentration Mode Activities for Students 28
    Low Concentration Mode Activities for Teachers 34
    Reflection Questions. 42

Chapter 3: Medium Concentration Mode 43
    Medium Concentration Mode Activities for Students 44
    Medium Concentration Mode Tasks for Teachers 50
    Reflection Questions. 54
        Daily Log 55

Chapter 4: High Concentration Mode 57
    High Concentration Mode Activities for Students 58
    High Concentration Mode Activities for Teachers 61
    Reflection Questions. 75
        Letter of Recommendation Request Form 76

Epilogue 77
References and Resources. 79
Index 89

ACKNOWLEDGMENTS

To Team Linnihan, the sounding board of all ideas. Thank you for always challenging me to be my best, to take chances, and to think big. To my four children—Madison, Sean, Ryan, and Michael—for remembering their time in school and pointing out what worked and what would make it better. To my dogs, who are surely smarter now as a result of listening to the classical music that has played throughout this entire process. To my husband, Patrick, for always pointing out what I do well, even if he is a bit biased. To my students, who sparked the light—and empathized with my deadlines!

Solution Tree Press would like to thank the following reviewers:

Lindsey Bingley
    Literacy and Numeracy Lead
    Foothills Academy Society
    Calgary, Alberta, Canada

Kelly Hilliard
    GATE Mathematics Instructor
      NBCT
    Darrell C. Swope Middle School
    Reno, Nevada

Christie Shealy
    Director of Testing and
      Accountability
    Anderson School District One
    Williamston, South Carolina

Elyse Webb
    Instructional Coach
    Dallas Center—Grimes CSD
    Grimes, Iowa

Visit **go.SolutionTree.com/teacherefficacy** to download the free reproducibles in this book.

ABOUT THE AUTHOR

Ellen I. Linnihan is a secondary English and public speaking teacher in the Elmbrook School District in Brookfield, Wisconsin. She is also an adjunct faculty member for the University of Wisconsin-Oshkosh Cooperative Academic Partnership Program (CAPP). Linnihan began her career teaching in Department of Defense schools in Kentucky and California. While raising four children, she spent ten years as a freelance writer for educational publishing companies.

Linnihan earned her National Board Certification for teaching secondary English in 2018. It was this experience that ignited a passion for sharing her ideas about creating a video archive to serve her students better. In addition to teaching, Linnihan is the program coordinator for the Distinguished Young Women of Brookfield scholarship program, a national program that develops and recognizes academic achievement, talent, and leadership in young women. She credits this program for launching her in a positive direction in life when she was a high school participant. In 2020, she was selected as one of the most influential educators in the Elmbrook School District. In 2022, she wrote *Capturing the Classroom: Creating Videos to Reach Students Anytime*, a Foreword Indies Honorable Mention award winner.

Linnihan earned her bachelor's degree in English and history from the University of Wisconsin-Madison. She furthered her studies at Austin Peay State University with a master's degree in education (curriculum and instruction) and a master's degree in English.

To learn more about Ellen's work, visit @EllenLinnihan on X, ellenlinni on Instagram, or www.capturingtheclassroom.com.

To book Ellen I. Linnihan for professional development, contact pd@SolutionTree.com.

INTRODUCTION

My Friday nights in Wisconsin as a kid meant one thing: roller-skating in the gym at my grade school. We lined up to rent skates for a quarter, laced up the relics that had never known WD-40, and rolled out into our equivalent of the Indy 500 auto race. The crashes were nearly as spectacular. The main event, however, was when the announcer, without any fanfare at all, let rip the song "Whip It" by Devo. Those of us who knew better elbowed our way as close to the start of the line at the center of the gym as possible. The unsuspecting newbies caught at the end of the line were in for a ride, and let me tell you, it never ended well for them. The whip was nothing if not predictable. After a few frantic revolutions, the people at the end flew mercilessly into the bleachers along the sides of the gym. Aside from a few bruises, it was harmless fun, though, right? Some might find this analogous to the teaching experience, but if this is how teaching feels to you, it's time to get off the whip!

The feeling of a force pulling you at an accelerated pace into impending doom is one that any rational person would try to dodge. Most teachers can relate to the dread of the upcoming unit that they know will consume them—the one that ends with a great big paper, project, portfolio, or other behemoth culminating summative assessment. You have just spent copious amounts of time teaching, coaching, mentoring, and cajoling the best possible work from your students, and then *they* are done. *You*, on the other hand, have a mountain to climb to get through the grading process. Many teachers have accepted this as a reality of the profession. It's why we get the summers off, right? Pay your dues as a stressed-out educator from September through June, and if you're lucky, then rehab your exhausted body and soul through the dog days of summer.

Taking command of your teacher time management enables you to prioritize your days so you can enjoy your evenings. Here's where modes of operation come in. Here, you learn to recognize and flow with the *modes of concentration*—another way of saying how much you must concentrate on tasks—that naturally occur. By recognizing and working on the tasks that correspond with how much you can concentrate for chunks of time throughout the workday, you will have more time to enjoy your personal life. The following introduction walks you through how this book aims to help you identify the modes in your teaching day and provide guidance for making the best choices to maximize your time.

What a Mode Is

Knowing how to manage ourselves—and our students—in a variety of modes is key to classroom survival. One sadly neglected aspect of teaching goals is quite often any recognition of the teacher's needs. Just like a factory has machines that require maintenance and fine-tuning for optimum performance, teachers need tweaking, too.

And I don't mean professional development.

What I mean is making our teaching experience so much more efficient that it makes the rest of life's aspects better, too. Who would turn down a better quality of life? More free time? Better relationships with colleagues? All of these factors have one common theme: stress. Consider the following data:

> Burnout is the top issue facing educators, with 90% of teachers calling the issue "very serious or somewhat serious." About 55% of teachers said they were considering leaving the field earlier than planned, with Black and Hispanic teachers even more likely to quit or retire. (GBAO, 2022, as cited Parrish, 2022)

The first step to prioritizing time well is to set your classroom goal. Then, you work toward achieving the classroom goal—whatever that may be—by

identifying and efficiently using different modes of operation. For the purposes of this book, there are three basic modes (Goldratt & Cox, 2012). Those three modes of concentration are (1) low, (2) medium, and (3) high. Teachers and students are always in one of these three modes but are not always in the same mode simultaneously. Different modes mean different levels of concentration and, therefore, different kinds of tasks. Different types of tasks require different levels of rigor, and each mode is best for doing certain types of tasks. This book helps you find ways to maneuver student modes so you can work to your greatest efficiency.

Gaining an understanding of each mode (described here) and the types of tasks to do in each helps you fine-tune your teacher time.

1. **Low concentration mode** is an ideal time to manage manual or repetitive teacher tasks, such as classroom maintenance or filing. Students in this mode may be working in groups or moving about the classroom.
2. **Medium concentration mode** is an ideal time for teachers to do small tasks that don't require deep thinking, close attention to detail, or an extended time period. This time may have similar constraints for students.
3. **High concentration mode** is the gold standard of time that is the most valuable for the teacher because it provides an opportunity to complete tasks that require deeper concentration. It is the mode that teachers experience the least, so recognizing it and using it appropriately will maximize teacher effectiveness in time management. For students, high concentration mode is generally spent in extended time periods for testing, writing, or reading independently.

Recognizing your current mode and your classroom's current mode will help you manage the situation with the best use of your time. When you function at maximum efficiency in all three modes, everything in the system improves the whole. It's simply a time management technique.

Why This Book

Time is one of the most valuable assets an educator possesses. It's also one of the main reasons teachers quit the profession (Walker, 2022). Teachers generally

put in many more hours than they are compensated for. You already know this, but here it is in black and white:

> While a school day is estimated to be around 6.7 hours, every educator knows that a teacher's workday is much longer. Add the time required for all the other parts of the job—lesson planning, providing students extra support, grading, and parent and staff meetings—and teachers can expect to put in a 12- to 16-hour workday. (Winters-Robinson, 2019)

Now, consider the fact that the longer you work, the less likely you are to be doing quality work:

> People are working so many hours that not only in most cases do they not have more hours they could work, but there's also strong evidence that when they work for too long, they get diminishing returns in terms of health costs and emotional costs. (Schwartz, as cited in Jabr, 2013)

Suppose for a moment, though, that you were able to slow things down. What would you do with a bit more margin in your life? Whether you revise instruction, spend more one-to-one time with students, focus on more detailed parent communication efforts, or take time for yourself, the extra minutes will fill quickly with the efforts you value most, making you a more balanced and effective educator.

That can happen because of the theory of constraints. Eliyahu M. Goldratt and Jeff Cox (2012), authors of *The Goal: A Process of Ongoing Improvement*, 40th Anniversary Edition, created a theory of constraints that provides simple steps focusing on the bottlenecks in any process and guidance that helps create a plan to make workflow smoother. This theory acknowledges that not all minutes are created equally. Some are more valuable than others because we are better able to concentrate during them. This book helps you identify the aforementioned different modes of operation—low-, medium-, and high-concentration times—and know the right type of work during each.

All you need are the tools to master your work time. This book gives you those tools.

About This Book

This book, for all K–12 teachers and paraprofessionals, helps you identify your *real* classroom goals. Your goal may be leading students to proficiency in a particular unit of content, such as identifying and understanding the various functions of the government, while your "real" goal may be instilling a sense of citizenship and conveying the workings of the government so they can actively participate in democracy. While these goals may seem interchangeable on the surface, the "real" goal focuses on internalizing knowledge. Both goals require time, and that means wisely managing that time—for both you and your students.

The chapters are organized as follows.

- Chapter 1 helps you identify your overarching classroom goal. Of course, some goals are mandated by curriculum standards, but others are broader or more holistic. Identifying what is most essential in the long run will determine what you do on a daily basis. You can get there faster by eliminating distractors and streamlining the process.
- Chapter 2 explains what low concentration mode looks like and how you and your students can most effectively use this time, which is one where students need a lot from you.
- Chapter 3 helps you through medium concentration mode, identifying the tasks that you and your students can accomplish most efficiently during this time. This is when your students will require some of your involvement but not complete guidance or interaction.
- Chapter 4 explores high concentration mode, which is when you can get the tasks done that require the most brain power and focus.

All chapters include Teacher Tips to call attention to tidbits that can improve the process, such as saving you time and helping students meet goals.

Every classroom has a rhythm—a pace or vibe in which energy is expended by both students and teachers. Feeling this rhythm and understanding the tempo is where you'll begin effectively using this approach, and the following chapters will help you identify and plan for this. You are already doing great work in your classroom. Now, take this growth opportunity to maximize your time. When you run on empty, everyone suffers—you, your family and friends, and your students.

CHAPTER 1
YOUR GOAL AND STREAMLINING

Each classroom has a unique atmosphere, largely led by the teacher's style, but any good classroom should have an overall goal that aligns with the building, district, and perhaps even government-mandated learning objectives. How a teacher leads students toward that goal can vary widely, but the goal itself should be common ground in classrooms of like subjects and levels.

Setting sights on the classroom goals will help you focus on what is truly necessary and helpful. For example, my class goal in a high school writing course may be to produce strong writers who can effectively command words so that they are focused and articulate. My process moves students toward that goal, focused on both the tangible work that they produce and the intangible learning. Many of the formative steps, although necessary and valuable, do not require the quality control measures that I use in assessing the final product. Written and verbal informal feedback moves students toward this goal. I don't, however, need to get lost in the details along the way. Neither do my students.

When considering your real goal, consider this: In an English language arts class, for example, *proficient writing* is the stated goal, but the "real" goal is *meeting objectives and managing time*.

Regardless of what grade, discipline, or proficiency level you teach, meeting your objectives on time is fundamental to your success as a teacher and your students' learning. The process that gets you to this goal will vary based on different factors, particularly your curriculum, but there are key fundamental truths that will support your efforts regardless of grade level or course content. The process includes identifying the goal, letting students know what the goal is, streamlining the process, and remaining fluid in your approach. However you get there, the goal remains the same.

Identify the Goal

What is the goal in your classroom? Is it specific knowledge? Is it skills based? If you are unsure, how can you lead students to the finish line? Distilling it into a single focus can be challenging.

Sixty percent of educators report using generative artificial intelligence (AI) to make their work more efficient (Hamilton, 2023). However, AI can also help make it easier to determine your overarching goal. To illustrate, I asked ChatGPT (https://chat.openai.com) to create a classroom goal for my Writing for College class. I inserted the entire school board-approved course documentation—standards, curriculum, and unit details—into the text box. My only additional prompt was *Condense it to one sentence*. The result perfectly synthesized the essence to the following: "The nine-week Writing for College English course aims to prepare college-bound students through refining writing skills, analyzing ideas, and developing tone, with a focus on essential understandings, alignment with standards, and diverse assessments, including a seven-week argumentative research project" (OpenAI, 2024).

While objectives meetings are generally friendly and focused, sometimes our individual visions don't mesh, and a turf battle threatens to erupt. I have participated in meetings that belabor the wording of a single policy for more than an hour. Especially when developing wording for a policy that will be included on every class syllabus (for example, a technology policy on cell phone use, AI, or other devices), buy in needs to be high. While some may bristle at the suggestion of resorting to AI, most of the time, everyone likes the focused language it produces based on all of our specific input. Ironically, AI is capable of generating specific policy language for the use of AI in student work.

If you don't use pre-provided state, provincial, or district standards to identify your goal, your building or district mission statement may also be a good place to start. My district, Elmbrook School District, located in Brookfield, Wisconsin, has the motto, "To inspire every student to think, learn, and succeed." This is broad, but if I take it unit by unit in my classroom, it works just by adding this context to the ending. For example, in a public speaking class, I may be teaching a business unit, including interview preparation, résumé writing, and the importance of timely and personalized thank-you notes. I could modify the goal to read: *To inspire every student to think, learn, and succeed in a business interview experience.*

This method works well at any level and for any subject area. Looking at elementary school literacy, for example, a grade 2 unit on writing could have a classroom goal that reads: *To inspire every student to think, learn, and succeed in a writing unit for a variety of modes to examine and convey complex ideas and information clearly and accurately.*

Let Students in on the Goal

Whatever grade level or subject you teach, your students benefit from knowing the goal and making connections between it and what you are currently asking of them (Midwest Comprehensive Center at American Institutes for Research, 2018).

In deciding how to bring the goal to the forefront for students, as well as yourself, consider the following questions.

- Do your students know why you are doing a particular lesson or activity?
- Do they know what they are supposed to know and be able to do for each unit?
- Do they have a clear understanding of how knowing and doing will take them closer to the overall classroom goal?

By internalizing the goal from the start of their effort, students take greater ownership, experience deeper learning, and exhibit self-efficacy (Midwest Comprehensive Center, 2018). When the goal is first and foremost in students' minds, it invites group buy-in. Researchers find that student academic performance improves with goal setting (Rowe, Mazzotti, Ingram, & Lee, 2017; Sides & Cuevas, 2020). Establishing a classroom learning goal makes students more likely to prioritize it rather than viewing it as merely the teacher's goal. As you convey the goal to students, what resonates with one student may not spark that light of learning in another. Providing as many ways as possible for students to visualize and internalize the goal increases the chance of success.

For example, some students prefer verbal directions, while others process information better when they can see an example. For units that I teach on a recurring basis, I post an Essential Documents folder on the online class learning platform. I include frequently asked questions, steps for accomplishing basic tasks, forms that students will use, and other helpful documents. I also share how-to videos for various steps in the process, and I link to student examples for those who prefer to see a good, finished product before starting. Providing a variety of supports through video tutorials and examples does two things: (1) gives students access to what *they* need to meet the classroom goals and (2) decreases the wait time they may otherwise have in seeking answers directly from you.

The best practices for informing students of each unit's goals are as follows (Kappa Delta Pi, 2022).

- Write them in student-friendly *I can* language.
- Point out the target when you begin a unit.
- Present the goal in text as well as verbally.
- Provide student exemplars.

The preceding practices don't take long after standards are rewritten in student-friendly language. Beyond that, it's a matter of briefly sharing in class. Some streamlining ideas follow to help facilitate your and your students' work toward your goal.

Determine Where You Can Streamline

Recognizing the mode of both you and your classroom environment can be a bit of a Goldilocks quest. Additionally, using the modes of operation to your advantage requires self-discipline. One way to develop discipline is to make a plan and decide where you can streamline. Coding the list by mode—those tasks that require low, medium, or high levels of concentration—makes it easier to select the most appropriate task to do when the time comes.

First, though, acknowledge that the perfect mode at the perfect time of the day with the perfect work to do is probably not going to occur often. The key is to recognize the mode for what it is and to take advantage of the opportunity to be productive. Selecting the right fit will keep you moving toward efficiency.

Remind yourself that following the demands of each mode requires discipline. For example, you may want to grade written assessments while students are working in groups, and that task may not be possible to do when the mood strikes or when you originally planned to do it because students may be in a low concentration mode that doesn't let you focus. If you try to review the assessments when students interrupt often (a low concentration mode identifier), it may take twice as long to complete the task. Choosing tasks that fit the best for each mode is far more important and time-saving than working directly through a to-do list.

Now, take a few moments and consider what work tasks you currently do outside of your scheduled work day. Your goal should be to fit them into the time in which you are paid. I say this fully understanding how impossible that sounds. Whatever you do, try not to fall victim to the *throbbing bag syndrome*:

> You take your bag home, full of all the best intentions, imagining an evening spent dealing with everything so you can start the next day on a clean slate. You bring in your bag, where it sits in the corner like a malevolent beast, and you don't touch it at all. But you never stop thinking about it. Get rid of throbbing bag syndrome by simply refusing to bring work home as a rule (accepting there are always times when this is not possible). (Happy Healthy Teacher, 2022)

This cycle of chock-full days and either work-filled evenings or a bag full of incomplete tasks making you feel anxious is almost always related to burnout, which takes its toll: "Teachers are leaving the field due to burnout at an alarming rate—8% a year. That is roughly 125,000 teachers who are too exhausted, frustrated and overwhelmed to stay in the classroom each year" (Moshman, n.d.). If you love to teach, I implore you to invest in *future you* by establishing sustainable work habits before you reach this point.

Really evaluate those tasks you bring home and consider whether you might break them down into low concentration mode tasks. This consideration and prioritization is a simple task that only requires low concentration to complete, which is a perfect example of how important low concentration mode focus can be. Taking the time to *plan* for your time keeps you on task in the future.

- **Are there tests with objective sections you could do piecemeal in those pockets of time?** Most of our bigger tasks consist of several steps, and not all of those steps require high concentration. For example, you may have a large assessment to grade that has both multiple-choice and short-response sections. Opening each test to the start of the multiple-choice section will get your pile organized for grading that section. If you are using a rubric to grade a lab report or essay, print and staple it to the assignment. Are there less time-intensive sections? If you can peck away at smaller tasks in low concentration mode, you can use your more valuable high concentration mode to do the tasks that require deeper thought.

- **Are you electronically entering grades outside of the school day?** There are ways to make this data entry task more manageable. Some professionals prefer to enter scores electronically after grading each assessment; for assessments such as speeches and presentations, this makes sense. However, consider printing a roster or keeping a hard copy to manually record scores to save time as you work your way through a stack of assessments. At the completion of grading, electronically entering scores while looking at an alphabetized printout is easier on the eyes and requires less time to search for names. Additionally, if you enter directly into the electronic gradebook for each student, there is the obvious temptation to visit other tabs on the computer. Add this to your ready-to-go low concentration mode tasks.

- **Are you checking homework or other formative work for completion only?** There is value in practice, but not everything a student completes requires a close reading. Consider saving time by spot-checking specific questions and adding brief but specific feedback or even a quick acknowledgment (*Creative* or *Precise*, for example). Consider that "grades are not the same as assessment" (Hough, 2023). If the assignment shows particular problem spots, focus on those and scan the rest.

Mode shifting is when you find yourself in a different mode of concentration than you anticipated or planned for. For example, you may be planning to grade essays while students watch a video but find that there is something more distracting going on that prevents a higher level of focus. Perhaps you thought a set of free-response essays would be straightforward and easy to assess, but instead, you find the responses unexpectedly engaging and insightful. A higher level of focus, requiring a deep level of concentration for analysis, might not be a good fit for the classroom activity at the moment. It could be that the video is more engaging for you, or you need to monitor students who are not paying attention.

Streamline the Process

With a goal in mind, all teachers have a vision of what their students can produce, demonstrate, or articulate at the end of a unit, class, or grade level. But the ultimate goal is really the *learning* that students internalize and carry to the next stage. Anyone who has taught the same concepts for years or even decades knows what it takes to move students toward that magical end of the rainbow. I am not suggesting that you sacrifice the quality of your instruction.

Instruction, of course, is directly related to feedback and all its various forms. Because research confirms that feedback is an element known to increase academic achievement, improve student attitudes toward a class, and positively affect student self-regulation skills (Ozan & Kincal, 2018), the following list addresses areas where you can finesse your practice so you can meet classroom goals and improve your quality of life at the same time.

- Formative one-to-one conferencing
- Peer-guided feedback
- Voice memo feedback
- Group-recorded feedback

Some up-front effort around these strategies will result in an ultimately more efficient set of systems.

Formative One-to-One Conferencing

One-to-one conferencing is the gold standard of feedback, as it allows for real-time clarification and relationship building that:

> allows students to build trust with their teacher and feel confident when asking questions. After receiving positive feedback from their teacher and getting the communication they need, students will be more prepared to ask questions throughout their schooling and careers. (Penney, 2024)

Obviously, this is time-consuming and must be done when your students are available. It also requires you to have a meaningful plan so other students can work independently while you focus on just one. Carving out time for personalized formative feedback, however, has a rich payoff. Following a protocol like the one outlined for a five-minute conference helps as well (ReDesign, 2021).

1. Assess each student's work, recording strengths and weaknesses. Record "concrete examples of each. (Make a copy to keep on file!)" (ReDesign, 2021, p. 8). For example, if using a rubric for a summative assessment, use this same rubric for the conference. Indicate to students in what areas they are currently demonstrating proficiency and which require further effort or reteaching. Formatively, you may want to focus on a first-step aspect of the rubric. For an essay, it may be something such as having a defensible thesis statement; this is a building block for the remainder of the essay. Whether this is an actual grade in your gradebook or simply a checkmark on a spreadsheet for future reference, both the teacher and students will be aware of whether the project is starting strong. Keeping a log reminds you who needs further support or direction to master this step, which will be essential in reaching the goal.
2. Tell students why you're conferencing with them. (For example, a simple rubric check-in will ensure that students and teachers have the same expectations for the final product.)
3. Your form, regardless of how else you customize it, should "Ask the student to explain the task in their own words" (so you can determine how well they understand the assignment) and require reflecting on their work, "possibly asking him or her to self-assess against a portion of the skills rubric" (ReDesign, 2021, p. 8).
4. Confer about the student's work. If using a rubric, reference those criteria and use specific examples.
5. Together, figure out the student's next steps to improve an area or two of growth.
6. Ask the student to "verbally summarize the key takeaway" to ensure they understand (ReDesign, 2021, p. 8).

The following ideas facilitate occasional feedback sessions such as these.

- **Keep it short:** A student conference can take as few as three minutes if both parties are prepared for it. That leads to the tools mentioned in the following item. Conferencing is easier to manage while students are working either independently or in small groups that do not require your direct instruction. Depending on the conference, student readiness may drive the timing. For example, if you are doing a midpoint check-in, in what order you see students is likely to be organically driven by when each has completed a stage of the process. If students are submitting something electronically, you can determine order based on who is ready to discuss work. Consequently, students who have already conferenced with you can help others by peer editing. This way, while you conference, students are actively moving toward their goals. These conferences may occur over several days.

- **Have students prepare for the conference prior:** Use a preconference form to gather the relevant focus points. For example, in my Writing for College class, I include a college prep unit to help students navigate the college application process. The students in that class complete the reproducible "College Planning Sheet" (page 22) ahead of the conference time. A simplified version, applicable for any unit or project at any level, appears in the reproducible "Preconference Form" (page 23). Pair either form with the assignment's rubric. This approach allows you both to focus on what matters—improvement in a specific area.

- **Run the conferences during class time when the students are focused on independent or small-group work:** To provide focus and, hopefully, avoid wasted time, students can turn over completed handwritten preconference forms or upload them onto the learning management system (such as Canvas) or a shared Google Doc when ready. Monitor the submissions, calling over students individually after they have submitted the form. You can visually cue students about the ongoing process by displaying the Google Docs on the SMART Board. Add student names to the document, share it with them, and ask them to link their document to their name when ready. After conferencing with someone, highlight their name on the document. Work through the list alphabetically or by seating chart so that they can anticipate their turn. This helps prevent anyone from lagging behind or missing the conferencing step.

Combine the five-step protocol from this section (or another that you prefer) with the provided guidance for formative conferences. Teaching students how to provide peer feedback is another way that students can hone their work prior to your conferences.

Peer-Guided Feedback

Taking the time to properly train students in the valuable lesson of giving constructive feedback is a solid investment. Research backs this investment, saying that, after learning how to provide and apply peer feedback, that feedback:

> can significantly improve students' writing ability and writing self-efficacy. At the same time, there is no significant difference

in the improvement of students' writing ability and writing self-efficacy after using peer feedback compared with those who receive teacher feedback. Secondly, as a result of the first point, the very labor-intensive teacher feedback can therefore be safely reduced and replaced by more scalable peer feedback. Thirdly, the use of peer feedback can promote the improvement of students' autonomous motivation in writing. (Cui, Schunn, Gai, Jiang, & Wang, 2021)

It's important for students to know exactly what they are assessing and how to assess. Giving them the same criteria that you will use to do the final evaluation will help them focus on the goal. For example, if the teacher provides an exact copy of the final grading rubric to use when doing peer evaluations, students can catch several issues, many of which are likely to be mechanical or formatting based (whether in a world language, art, history, or science lab class). Those are details that even a struggling student can point out as missing or incorrect. It's important to encourage students to have as many peer editors as they can find to give them feedback. The more eyes on the work in progress, usually, the better the final product.

- **Provide sentence starters:** They give students a launching point. Beginning with an "I like, I wish, I wonder framework . . . [helps] focus students on content rather than grammar and spelling errors" (Tutt, 2021). Other examples follow.
  + *I think what you are trying to say is . . . am I understanding this correctly?*
  + *Have you considered . . . ?*
- **Provide a rubric:** List criteria and request ratings, or ask specific questions and require that respondents provide explanations. For example, the tool could ask, "What terms or concepts did the author fail to adequately explain?" and "How can the author improve the use of sources" (Gehringer, 2017, p. 3)?
- **Ask peer reviewers to answer three questions:** The description part of the feedback is nonevaluative, which can help lower students' guard and helps students understand if they're giving readers what they need (Eli Review, n.d.).
  + *Describe*—What do you see as a reader?
  + *Evaluate*—How does the text meet or not meet the criteria established in the prompt?
  + *Suggest*—What concrete advice for improvement do you have?

Even with this guidance, students sometimes provide low-effort feedback because they are in a hurry or simply don't buy into the value of the process. To prevent these flyby feedback patterns, you can require students to complete a tool such as the reproducible "Peer Edit Rubric—Argument Research Paper" (page 24), which provides thoughtful prompts, and "Peer Analysis Form" (page 26), which gives you insight into the value of the feedback. I emphasize that the feedback they collect is their own responsibility.

If a peer gives superficial comments such as *Great job* or *This is an A!*, the recipient needs to ask the reviewer to dig deeper. Suggest editing one paragraph "for clarity and conciseness. Suggest other paragraphs that could benefit from the same revisions" (Writing Across the Curriculum Clearinghouse, n.d.). Providing conversation starters like the following can also help (McDonald, n.d.; Slinkman, 2023; Writing Across the Curriculum Clearinghouse, n.d.).

- **Read or look carefully at the work.**
    + What I take from this is _____.
    + In light of our assignment, _____ makes sense.
    + Does my understanding of _____ match your intention?
- **Point to specific issues.**
    + I could use more detail here: _____.
    + This felt like a big jump in sequence: _____. This might help: _____.
    + A source or example here would help: _____.
- **Mention the strongest part of the work.**
    + You _____ really well.
    + The _____ worked because _____.

After receiving successful feedback from a peer, a student is more likely to ask that person for help again. If I see that someone was not helpful, I can intervene and give that student more specific guidance about giving helpful feedback.

Requiring peer feedback not only helps improve the writing they are critiquing but there is also evidence that the act of peer editing can help improve the editor's (or art critic's) work, as well. The process of critiquing someone else's work "helps students develop lifelong skills in assessing and providing feedback to others, and also equips them with skills to self-assess and improve their own work" (Center for Teaching Innovation, n.d.).

Voice Memo Feedback

Making feedback as accessible as possible is important, so consider these reasons for recording your spoken feedback.

- You don't have to worry about students being able to read your handwriting.
- Most people can speak much faster than they can write or type.
- Alternative feedback modes, including audio recordings, help improve student comprehension because of the teacher's inflection and tone of voice (Killingback, Drury, Mahato, & Williams, 2020).
- Audio (as well as video and computer-assisted) instructional feedback is one of the most effective feedback forms (Fancourt, 2018; Hattie & Timperley, 2007).
- This feedback delivery method improves teacher-student relationships by conveying a tone that students appreciate (Kirwin, Raftery, & Gormley, 2023).

Some word-processing programs have voice memo capabilities built into them so that you can insert comments where necessary. A simplified method, however, is to record a voice memo on your phone and share the file with the student. If your classroom uses Zoom (or a similar video-conferencing tool), you can video record your screen as you scroll through a document and respond verbally. Read the assignment (either aloud or silently to yourself), leaving feedback on the recording as you respond organically to the text. Make sure to let students know where you are in their work before you begin the feedback audio. Then, save the file and share it with the student.

The biggest question whenever considering if making a change is worth the shift is *will it work*? According to one study, "Students who received audio feedback were three times more likely to apply the contents of audio feedback to subsequent work" (Ice, Curtis, Phillips, & Wells, 2007, as cited in Stuart, 2020). That is compelling!

Group-Recorded Feedback

While not exactly personalized, there are times when giving feedback to a group about a particular assignment can be powerful. For example, in my AP language class, the students practice writing rhetorical analyses in which they analyze the same text by a given writer. Addressing the group as a whole and pointing out common mistakes or misinterpretations can be comforting to some in a "We're all in this together" sort of way.

Often, I record my audio group feedback to share with the class before returning their individual essays. By making one general feedback recording, I can cover a range of issues that many students encountered at one time. The recording may only be a few minutes. Recording (writing or saying) it for each student individually could take an hour or more. After playing the feedback video in class, I invite students to look over their work to find these issues. Once students have heard the general feedback, they are often more prepared to hear their specific feedback. If, after receiving both types of feedback, they still don't understand how or where they went adrift, I encourage them to pop in for a five-minute conference to discuss their particular paper. These cases are infrequent because they have already received clear feedback twice.

It's much easier to accommodate occasional one-to-one conferencing with these prior steps in place. Keeping that teacher time in mind, you won't regret the time it takes to provide group feedback if it results in less time providing additional personalized feedback. Considering the goal, use the tools that help you achieve it with the least amount of investment of your time.

Homework

Considering your own time starts with considering your students' time. Assigning only what is necessary and aligned with learning outcomes that meet the overarching goal is key. The reality is that the more work you create for your students, the more work you create for yourself—but the amount is exponential. Enter the age-old conundrum: assign homework? You might have a preference, so might your administrator, and so might your district. You'll have to work within those confines.

If you must assign homework or believe it is worth having students do it, align assignments with researched guidelines: ten minutes per grade level per night (Good & Brophy, 2003; National Education Association, 2019). And keep in mind that five classes assigning, for example, 120 minutes of homework a night results in ten hours of homework in one evening for a senior. What too much homework does to students has a "plethora of evidence that it's detrimental to their attitude about school, their grades, their self-confidence, their social skills and their quality of life" (Donald-Pressman, as cited in Wallace, 2015).

If you're on the fence, have agency about how much homework to assign, and want to make an informed decision, consider the research: "The link between homework and student achievement is far from clear. There is no conclusive evidence that homework increases student achievement across the board" (Serna, 2021).

Remind yourself of your overarching goal. Then, determine whether you can reach it if students don't do homework. In my class, I would argue that they cannot reach the goal without doing the assigned reading, which is one reason I read aloud to my secondary students in class. The benefits are numerous across writing, reading, and comprehension skills and attitudes, and overall, read alouds improve academic achievement in the long run (Mol & Bus, 2011; Ness, 2024).

If the goal drives the focus, that matters more than qualms about "lowering" the standards. If, for example, the true goal in your classroom is for improved reading capabilities—comprehension, aptitude, and accuracy—the goal may be more complex than it appears on the surface. Teaching these skills will likely move students in the right direction, but infusing a *love* for reading generates student buy-in, which is a key component to reaching any goal. For a deeper dive into this topic, visit www.youtube.com/watch?v=kHqw5IS-3Vc to watch the Capturing the Classroom: A Convo With Ellen Linnihan episode on George Couros's (2021) *The Innovator's Mindset Podcast*.

Be Fluid

In my early days of teaching, my lesson plans were thorough, detailed, and planned to the minute. I felt a sense of empowerment and comfort knowing exactly what I wanted to teach and accomplish in any given class. While I still feel that this is a great confidence builder and generally good practice, anyone who has spent more than a day in a classroom knows that the best lesson plans do not always stay on track. There was a time when I felt that this was a sign of a flop. Either we didn't make it through the entire lesson, or I found myself getting creative halfway through the period, trying to find ways to fill the remaining time. In reality, both of these scenarios are inevitable and really not so bad.

Flexible teaching is "an approach to both teaching and curriculum design that acknowledges" learners' changing needs and is a better and more realistic approach (Ripiceanu, 2023). It allows you to focus on the goal and move students in that direction (Ripiceanu, 2023). With the class goal in mind, "teachers who are flexible in how they schedule their class time can" achieve the tough ideal of addressing the "needs of students from diverse cultural, socio-economic, and linguistic backgrounds" (Ripiceanu, 2023). This flexible mindset allows you, as the teacher, to adjust the pace. There is no shame in moving faster or slower than you anticipated when planning. The key is to continue moving toward the goal in the most effective and efficient way possible.

Being flexible or fluid allows teachers to maximize time. Essentially, keeping a finger on the pulse of what students need in the moment has a greater impact on learning than sticking to a lesson plan:

> [Students'] most-positive experiences depended more on the number of opportunities for student-instructor interaction than on the type of

learning environment itself. How instructors and students organized and spent class time, and the amount of feedback and direct interaction, mattered more than the use of technology. (Cohn, 2021)

Technology in education may have a questionable reputation, but technology itself is not inherently negative. Context is everything. If instruction is meaningful and successfully leads students toward their learning goals, the delivery method may not be relevant—especially if technology allows more teachers to positively impact more students. Videos are one of the most efficient and time-saving instructional delivery methods. Using videos allows students to take the extra time where needed to reinforce learning without affecting the class lesson or teacher's timeline. For example, if a student needs additional instruction on a specific step and you have recorded the lesson on video, you can direct the student to that resource. It does not cause the entire lesson to come to a halt. Once students get a refresher, they can jump right back into the class. The same goes for absent students and those who benefit from repeated instruction.

Understanding student needs requires a high level of focus (corresponding with the high mode of concentration). A wealth of resources available to students can make this less time consuming in the long run. Videos are just one such resource. Exemplars and FAQ documents are also great resources, as mentioned. In this way, you can work in the most efficient mode (and you learn about the modes in the forthcoming chapters and what work corresponds with each) and move your students toward the classroom goal. Keeping the focus on the classroom goal by adjusting to learning needs and pushing forward when possible maximizes student learning and teacher effectiveness.

Reflection Questions

In light of this chapter, consider the following questions.

- If I were able to carve out an additional hour of time in my day for myself, how would I spend it?
- In my recent teaching experience, were there times when I felt out of control or out of sync with the classroom clock? What was I trying to accomplish when I felt this way?
- When was the last time I took a good look at my homework assignments to determine if they were the best way to help students reach their goals? Can I trim anything?
- Am I making the best use of feedback from peers to reduce my own time grading?
- What could I record and offer as video to students?

College Planning Sheet

My name:	
I have already applied to colleges:	
Yes, totally done	
Started, but I need to work on it	
No, I need to get started	
No, I am taking a gap year or doing something else amazing	
My dream college:	

College	Application deadline	Common Application?	Essay required?	Recommendation letters required?	Counselor letter of recommendation?	Accepted?

Scholarships	Application deadline	Essay required?	Letters of recommendation required?	Received or rejected

Letters of recommendation	Essays	Word count

I would like guidance about this:

Preconference Form

My name:

Before we start, I want my teacher to know this about my assignment:

My assignment was to:

In my assignment, my greatest strength was:

In my assignment, my greatest area for growth was:

I would like help understanding how to improve on:

Peer Edit Rubric–Argument Research Paper

Writer's Name:	Peer Editor's Name:

Ideas

- Is the thesis clear and focused?
- Does the writer sufficiently address the counterargument?
- Does the writer build to the strongest argument?
- Are there relevant, quality details to support the thesis?
- Does the writer stay on topic or drift off? If they drift off, where does it occur?
- Does the paper meet the length requirement?

Organization

- How does the writer hook the reader?
- Are there strong topic sentences that clearly support the thesis?
- Are there thoughtful, clear transitions?
- Does the order of the information make sense?
- Is the title original and interesting?
- Is there a strong conclusion that restates the thesis, leaving no loose ends?

Voice

- Is the tone appropriate, showing interest or enthusiasm for the topic?
- Are there any forms of first or second person (I, me, my, our, us, we, you, your)?
- Is the tone professional throughout the paper?
- Are there any contractions?
- Are there any generalizations (thing, a lot, lots, "Did you know", "Have you ever wondered")?
- Is there any passive voice?

Word Choice

- Is the writing specific and accurate, leading to a clear understanding?
- Are there striking words and phrases that catch the reader's eye?
- Are the language and phrasing appropriate for the audience?
- Does the tense stay the same throughout?
- Is there subject-verb agreement?
- Is there pronoun agreement?
- Are lists parallel?

Sentence Fluency

- Are the sentences consistently clear, correct, and easy to understand?
- Are there fragments or run-ons?
- Are there clear and strong transitions?
- Are there quotes that are not connected fluently to the paper with the writer's own words?

Conventions

- Does the writer need to work on spelling?
- Is punctuation accurate?
- Is capitalization accurate?
- Does the writer need to work on grammar and usage?
- Does the paper follow the correct format?
- Are quotes and citations correct?
- Are author, title, date, and publication always included?
- Are there a minimum of two citations not from a website?
- Has the writer included a bibliography?
- Do the citations in the paper match those in the bibliography?

Comments

Peer Analysis Form

My name:
Name of first peer editor:
I chose this editor because:
My editor was really helpful in this way:
I would use this peer editor again (select one):
No thank you　　　　　　Maybe　　　　　　Definitely
Name of second peer editor:
I chose this editor because:
My editor was really helpful in this way:
I would use this peer editor again (select one):
No thank you　　　　　　Maybe　　　　　　Definitely

Teacher Time Management © 2025 Solution Tree Press • SolutionTree.com
Visit **go.SolutionTree.com/teacherefficacy** to download this free reproducible.

CHAPTER 2
LOW CONCENTRATION MODE

One of my favorite things to do is drive my 2003 manual transmission Toyota Spyder convertible, which I lovingly refer to as Charlotte. When I drive her, there is absolutely nothing else I can do except shift gears. My phone is tucked away, and there is no chance to sip coffee. To drive Charlotte requires complete focus and knowing when to adjust the gear. I would say that the biggest challenge in learning to drive a stick shift is not so much in knowing how to shift but in knowing *when* to shift. Recognizing pace and shifting to meet it is key in the classroom, as well. There may not be posted speed limits in your room, but other signs will cue you when that classroom engine is revving up, and with practice, you learn how to flexibly shift.

The first gear is low concentration mode. During low concentration mode, students are occupied with self-paced activities that require minimal guidance but a good deal of supervision. The best time to complete tasks in low concentration mode is when you do not have enough time to accomplish anything intensive. These moments can, for example, happen when a lesson comes to an earlier-than-anticipated close or when a brief activity takes a few moments longer than planned. You will get experienced at spotting these opportunities. You will start grabbing scraps of time to knock out small but essential tasks throughout your day. For example, the last class in a high school day often sinks into a poor habit of packing up earlier than the previous classes. Students are understandably anxious to end the day, get to practice, and so on. On the other hand, teaching right up to the bell can feel chaotic and unsatisfactory if you are cut off by the bell every day. This is when low concentration mode activities can work the best.

You might even think of low concentration mode as downtime. That downtime offers benefits for you and your students: "Beyond renewing one's powers of concentration, downtime can in fact bulk up the muscle of attention—something that scientists have observed repeatedly in studies on meditation" (Jabr, 2013). This mode typically lasts fifteen minutes or fewer, so think of it as a power surge opportunity. If you are prepared for it and ready to hit the ground running, you can do quality work in this time.

An important thing to remember as you enter this chapter is that recognizing when your classroom is in low concentration mode and adjusting your expectations accordingly is imperative. Match that energy. Although it's tempting to think, *What can I get done right now?* while the students are occupied, selecting the right task is key to squeezing the most productivity possible out of your teacher time. In the past, I may have thought that I could grade a few essays while students worked in small groups, but that was a complete mode mismatch. Generally speaking, when students are in low concentration mode, you should be, too. Papers require concentration and deserve attention for meaningful and constructive comments. Not only would I be doing my students an injustice by giving them less than my full attention to assess, but I would be neglecting the students in my classroom during that time. Providing verbal formative feedback during the writing process is a better match for the mode than attempting to do high concentration mode activities such as grading student summative projects or papers.

Read on for low concentration mode activities for students and teachers.

Low Concentration Mode Activities for Students

When the classroom is in low concentration mode, it does not mean that no one is working. Some of the best work may be happening in pockets of activity all over the room. In fact, "students who were given a mundane task to complete after learning something new were better able to retain the information compared to those [who] were given something else to remember immediately after" (Hemmingson, 2019).

That means that mixing in some tasks that require small amounts of concentration after some tough lessons can be helpful.

You might initially feel uncomfortable with the low concentration mode because you are concerned that your students may be off task. And if they are—a small portion of the time—that's OK! Just because those moments are not producing tangible assessment material doesn't mean they lack value or are unnecessary. They're not just incorporating information into their memories but building positive relationships with each other, which can result in the following benefits.

- Practice of intrapersonal skills like self-regulation (Cervantez & Gutierrez, 2019; Pepler & Bierman, 2018)
- Practice of interpersonal skills like seeking to understand peer perspectives (Cervantez & Gutierrez, 2019; Pepler & Bierman, 2018)
- Improved school attendance (National Center on Safe Supportive Learning Environments, n.d.)
- Increased overall engagement, including participation in class (Juvonen, Espinoza, & Knifsend, 2012)
- Increased sense of belonging in school (Osterman, 2023; Yibing, Lynch, Kalvin, Liu, & Lerner, 2011)

In essence, letting students talk may help build community, so don't sweat those moments when students appear to be temporarily off task. Providing the framework and gently reminding your students of the goal will help to keep distractions to a minimum and keep everyone moving in the right direction.

Students may be doing a variety of tasks completely unrelated to one another (especially in a secondary classroom such as study hall), and their needs may vary greatly from requiring no teacher input to needing one-to-one help. Remaining flexible and responsive to student needs is key. If you have your mind set on accomplishing a task that requires your full concentration, it's easy to get frustrated when you must stop to engage with students who are struggling, which isn't fair to them. You will not complete your planned task, but you will also miss out on the opportunity to knock out some low concentration mode tasks of your own, creating unwanted homework for yourself.

Consider the process of making sugar cookies with cookie cutters. Anyone who has done this knows one thing to be true: there will always be scraps of dough left over after you cut out the shapes. What do we do with those scraps? As a kid, I ate my fair share of them. My mother's signature move was to shape the scraps into the first letter of our names to make a personalized cookie for each of us. Other people roll together the scraps to create a new surface for more cookie cutting. Whether you eat the scraps, form them freehand, or turn them into fresh cutouts, the point is that the margin between the "real" cookies has value. The time students spend chatting about personal interests is the equivalent of the dough scraps. Just as the cutters will never line up perfectly, the projects, skill practice, and so on will never progress without this kind of in-between. Sometimes, the scraps are the best! Take advantage of this margin to help forge better relationships in your classroom.

You likely manage a classroom that shifts quickly from moments of complete focus to moments of complete chaos. Riding that ebb and flow successfully takes practice. Set the expectation that students rein in their social time when you have indicated it's time to focus. In my public speaking class, the moments between the speeches are spent in low concentration mode. In a short window of time—approximately two minutes—my students will take care of their personal business in a variety of ways. Most will be handwriting formative feedback for the previous speaker, then delivering the notes to their desks. Others may have missed the previous speech because they were watching a video of their own speech in the hallway and completing a self-evaluation form. Some will be shuffling through notecards in preparation for their upcoming speech. When the speaker is ready, however, the chaos comes to a quiet close, and the focus is back on the podium.

Without direction, some students might waste this opportunity to complete tasks in low concentration mode, failing to recognize the opportunity to use those scraps of time wisely. It is important to guide students to do appropriate tasks during this time, too. This is a time to take care of small tasks requiring little concentration. Students, for example, should not be writing their speeches during these brief intervals. Most students use these scraps of time to upload their visual links, complete self-evaluations, or provide feedback to peers.

 Let students know that missing the chance to take care of business during this time could result in unintended homework or missing assignments.

You may set aside time for the open-ended choice of which task to perform during this time, or you may advise students to notice and efficiently use such downtime.

Examples of low concentration mode activities for students follow.

- Working in small groups or with partners (including student presentations)
- Doing seat work (including computer tutorials, worksheets, and the like)
- Doing test preparation or revisions from a recent assessment

The following sections provide some further ideas for when students are working on projects and so on.

Working in Small Groups and With Partners

When students are working on presentations, jigsaws, and the like—either in pairs or in groups—they can work on tasks that require low concentration. Students tend to love this mode because it is more relaxed and often allows for more communal chitchat. You can shift the focus to low concentration mode when appropriate with statements like, "You have ten minutes to check in with your groups or check off low-priority tasks for your projects." This type of cue will automatically signal low gear.

It's important to recognize that not all small-group and partner work time is designated as appropriate for low concentration mode, as some such work is likely to require medium concentration, especially for substantial assessments.

Consider the following as you plan when you might do low concentration mode tasks.

- There are many points of focus, as opposed to a singular point (when you may be conducting a whole-class lesson, for instance). Elementary students may be at the end of an art lesson that requires them to clean up and return supplies; a high school chemistry class may be finishing experiments and cleaning equipment.
- The instruction or classroom structure may be looser in the sense that everyone is working on a common task, but not everyone is at the same point in the project, and they may be concentrating on others' work rather than their own. As long as students are aware of and focused on the goal, however, a looser atmosphere can be productive.
- You are likely circulating the room to monitor and having off-the-cuff conversations. Circulating around the classroom ensures that students are on task and allows you to gather and provide formative feedback about the task.

Because you are being flexible, your task doesn't *always* need to be the same concentration level as your students'. Depending on your class, this may be the perfect time for you to do a medium concentration mode task, such as providing one-to-one feedback to students. When that feels like an impossible scheduling task, using these moments to do it in a small-group setting may be the perfect fit:

> Small groups make it easy for teachers to give students the one-on-one attention they need, to observe their learning in action, and to provide constructive feedback. Students take personalized feedback and use it during whole class instruction and when doing homework, so the result is improved student outcomes. (Francis, 2022)

As mentioned, whether you can incorporate this medium concentration mode task depends on your students. If students suspect you will not notice if they get off course, they are likely to do just that. Remaining present in the moment is key to keeping your students on track. This makes a task requiring high concentration a poor fit for when students are in low concentration mode. Even if you can accomplish it, it is unlikely for students to stay on track without your guidance and monitoring. You are not unlike a traffic light in this situation: When it goes out, chaos is likely to ensue rather quickly. However, if your students are generally highly self-directed, you may be able to dip into medium concentration tasks—but you still need to monitor their focus. If not (because you are unable to monitor them or they don't stay on task, or both), you might need to stick to low concentration mode tasks yourself.

Of course, you may have just one or two students who struggle to focus alone or in a small group. Positioning yourself near them can let them feel your presence when working, which can help them stay on task. A monitoring system for student computers in your room is another way to keep an eye on student work. For example, I can display my students' computer screens on a monitor at my desk. The control settings allow me to block specific websites and make others preferential. If a student is on a website that is unrelated to the task at hand, I can freeze the computer or send a direct message asking the student to get back on track.

Doing Test Preparation or Revisions From a Recent Assessment

One of the best ways to personalize learning is by allowing students the opportunity to review assessment materials for a test, retest, or project redo. Test preparation can take many forms, from independent work to whole-class review games. One of the best ways to prepare for a reassessment in low concentration mode is to spend time reviewing concepts not understood by the majority of the class.

Students partnering to review can strengthen both students' knowledge. Whether a student is learning from another student's explanation or doing the explaining, the concepts will grow stronger for both students (Weimer, 2018).

Reviewing and recalling reinforce knowledge, so redos are something to embrace (Paul, 2016; Wiklund-Hörnqvist, Jonsson, & Nyberg, 2014)—and perhaps your school has already embraced proficiency-based grading in which students must keep working to achieve learning goals until they meet them. Having students explain concepts to each other will help all students focus on the goal and build knowledge while reducing the amount of time you need to spend regrading. That results in more low concentration mode time for yourself, and their work will result in less work for you to do when you assess the work produced as a result of their partnered review. The biggest benefit is that the students will also be learning more and moving closer to the goal.

Periodic practice tests followed by a deep dive into the concepts that students have missed is also a time you can accomplish a low concentration mode task. Spending time addressing the entire class for each question review would be time-consuming for you and the students who already comprehend. Students can independently or in small groups examine the missed questions to learn the rules and internalize them for the next time; they can use an explanation guide for the incorrect responses. For those questions that a small group missed in common, a peer who got the answer correct can explain it in a personalized, focused effort to those students who struggled with that same item.

While students are engaged in this peer-to-peer review, you can circulate the room to check for comprehension and evaluate areas that surface as problematic for many students. Taking note of these sticking points will help you plan a different instruction for the concept. That may mean creating a tutorial video or simply interrupting the session to do a quick reteach of the concept to the full group. To ensure that students are productive during this time, employ the reproducible "Peer Analysis Form" (page 26). This holds students accountable and provides a framework for them to focus on the goal.

Students also can silently or with peers review teacher feedback on a written assessment (an essay, for example) and read samples from other students with commentary from either the teacher or an other provided source (such as an exemplar from the College Board or ACT organization). Seeing examples of how someone else approached the same writing prompt can be eye opening for a struggling student; they can see what observations and evidence others used to build their own arguments and improve their approach in the future (Hawe, Dixon, & Hamilton, 2021).

I create a slide to project in the classroom during low concentration mode that lists the day's to-dos. Displaying it is a subtle, friendly reminder of what students can do during this time. I don't need to distract the full class and interrupt their focus by making a big announcement that they may or may not acknowledge. When a student is in an independent flow state, interrupting with an unrelated announcement could bounce right off of them or distract them from making progress. Displaying it for all to see gives them a visual cue when they are ready to process it. Think about doing this when giving a test, as well. Inevitably, students finish at different times, leaving the early birds with nothing to do. This often leads to unwanted whispering and movement that can be distracting to others still focused on the assessment. By displaying a to-do list on the board, students can seamlessly move into the next task and not waste time just sitting and waiting for others to finish.

Low Concentration Mode Activities for Teachers

During low concentration mode activities, students may frequently ask questions of you. Your ability to concentrate will be challenged, so your productivity with tasks that require deep concentration will be limited. While you may occasionally be able to knock out a medium mode task if the class is highly self-directed or very small, these opportunities are infrequent. Just as you want tasks in the low concentration mode ready for your students, it's best to have your go-to list of low concentration mode tasks ready to tackle to make the most of the minutes.

Tasks that fall into this category are low-effort, often manual, tasks—those that result in something you can see. If you are interrupted mid-task, which you likely will be if you are truly in low concentration mode, you can easily jump in and out of it so that you're offering students the support they need to further their learning. These are often the neglected tasks or those you have relegated to a free afternoon or weekend. If you have them ready to knock out, they are a perfect fit for low concentration mode in your already full day.

Examples of low concentration mode activities for teachers follow.

- Self-care activities
- Sorting and otherwise organizing (supplies, for instance)
- Filing, laminating, sharpening pencils
- Moving desks, tidying, decorating

- Leading brain breaks
- Inventorying (books or supplies, for example)
- Creating electronic copies on your computer
- Building community for social-emotional learning activities
- Entering grades
- Copying and pasting communications (preparing a weekly email, duplicating a survey, and so on)
- Updating a class communication platform

The following sections provide some further ideas for when students are completing low concentration mode tasks, and you can do so as well.

Taking Care of Yourself

Rather than viewing self-care as a luxury you can't afford, consider caring for yourself as an investment in your practice; it is pivotal to caring for your health and well-being (Minshew, 2023). Instead of waiting for the "right" time to take care of yourself, use low concentration mode: "Don't wait for the 'big' break to pour back into you, start now" (Jackman, 2024). In fact, "approaching self-care in small, bite-sized activities" is more likely to lead to long-term habit changes (Jackman, 2024). Consider opportunities in your daily life to ease the stress. Low concentration mode is the perfect time to incorporate brief moments of self-care.

What does this look like in the classroom? You may have different needs depending on the grade level you teach, but everyone will benefit from occasional brain breaks (Jorgenson, 2023). In my high school classroom, I call it a *wiggle break*. Students are allowed to get up and move around for five minutes halfway through the period. You might lead a quick stretch or yoga session. Whatever works for you, consider that your students likely need breaks, too. A quick reset can help everyone focus better when it's time to get back to work.

Organizing Tangible Items

When my own children were young and begging to put up decorations at home for the holidays, my response was always the same at the start: "You can't decorate a mess." Organization is necessary to function. This is also true when you lose something, which leads to the truth that the best way to find something is to clean up.

Keeping a well-organized environment will benefit your mental health. This is true for all teachers. For example, science teachers have beakers, slides, and chemicals; music teachers wrangle instruments, chairs, sheet music, and stands; and physical education teachers have sports equipment of all kinds to manage. Each teacher has a domain to maintain. Building routine tasks for organizing and maintenance into the classroom expectations will help save your teacher time. An organized classroom also increases your professional self-efficacy (Larson, 2022) and reduces disruptions (Kelly, 2020). Don't neglect your students' role in supporting an organized classroom. It's important to also direct them to stay on task and put things back from where they retrieved them.

Organizing Digital Content

Some tasks are admittedly more enjoyable than others. Personally, I thrive when my electronic files are organized. The time that I used to spend searching for files that I had not clearly labeled or filed I will never get back. Now, I am freakishly devoted to maintaining my Google Drive. My husband, a West Point graduate, often shares with me the tales of the room inspections at the U.S. Military Academy. Every item had its place, and every room had identical inventory. He recalls it as torture, but to me, it sounds like perfection.

If you haven't already, once you have discovered the beauty of organizing folders, you can efficiently search for what you need. For each class that I teach, I have a folder that contains unit and administrative folders. In each admin folder, I have folders for each term (year) that I have taught it. Figure 2.1 is an example of folder organization, but your setup will vary according to what you teach and how your brain works.

One benefit of organizing this way is easy access to specific student data. For example, by sending a survey to request topic selections for speeches and papers, I have a great resource to share with future students who need ideas. I can easily share this document by linking it to my "Week at a Glance" document.

On the particular day that the topic selection is due, students can access the form to request a topic, see the topics that others in the class have already selected, and view the topics that a previous class has chosen under *Need Ideas?* Taking just a moment to link to these data gets students moving in the right direction faster and without your direct instruction.

In the past, I might have had fifteen two- to three-minute conversations with individual students who were struggling to select a topic. Now, it is rare that anyone needs this individualized attention for this purpose. The time it takes to post a hyperlink is negligible, but the time-saving impact can be immeasurable. All of these steps safeguard your teacher time, but even more importantly, if you use low concentration mode to post it while you have an open minute or two, you won't have to do it later. Taking advantage of doing small but important tasks during low concentration mode will have a time-saving effect on your teacher time in the future.

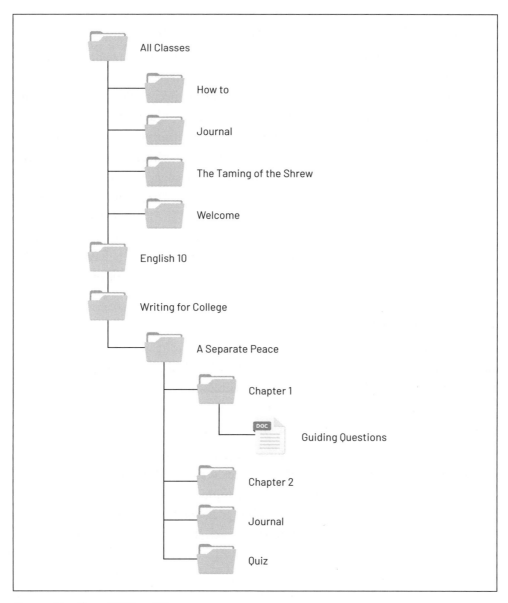

Source: Linnihan, 2022, p. 79.

FIGURE 2.1: Folder setup.

 Letting go of the idea that you need a complete block of time to complete a task is the first step in taking control of low concentration mode. Don't wait for the perfect moment to tackle a task from start to finish. Doing that most likely leads to you doing it on your own (unpaid) time. Split it apart and use the scraps of time.

Building Community for Social-Emotional Activities

Students tend to interact more during this mode, which can make connecting on a personal level easier or more likely for them. Because it's difficult to find the time to do targeted SEL work, take advantage of low concentration mode to pursue that community building. Doing so can work to students' and your advantage for the classroom goal, since improved belonging leads to improved academic achievement as well as improved emotional and mental health and behaviors (Allen, Gray, Baumeister, & Leary, 2022). Use this time to engage students in "specific evidence-based programs that target skills related to self-care, resiliency, social connectedness, managing stressors, and resolving conflict" (Allen, Vella-Brodrick, & Waters, 2016). What this looks like in your classroom will be unique. For elementary students, you may display anchor charts showing prosocial behaviors. At the secondary level, it may take a more personal or subtle form like journaling.

Creating Weekly Agendas

Like several tasks you can do during this time, up-front work pays dividends in the long run. Along with organizing files, acting in advance pays off. Weekly agendas are a way to communicate expectations with families, address student inquiries before ten of them ask the same question, and offer accessible resources to minimize the questions you get that can be answered through those resources.

When you have the district calendar for the upcoming school year, along with your teaching schedule, you can create a weekly agenda for each class or course. After you have done this once, you can make copies of your current agendas, revise them as needed to reflect refreshed learning goals, and then adjust the in-service and holiday dates in the future so they are correct. This process might take me two school days to complete, using moments of available classroom time. For example, you can use a Google slide show for a weekly document for each course. Select a background color and when copying the document for the new term, select a new background color. Change it one slide at a time as you update with the correct dates. Changing the color scheme to reflect the new school year based on the weeks completed is an easy way to jump right back into the work each time and not lose your place in the process.

Figure 2.2 is an example of a weekly agenda, and it includes links to recordings I have made of lectures and class discussions (for students who want to go over content again, have specific accessibility needs, or were absent) and a daily fun question. Visit **go.SolutionTree.com/teacherefficacy** to access a free reproducible template that you can customize.

Teacher: Linnihan	
Contact information linnihan@teacher.k12.school.edu Room 212 Office hours: Tuesday through Friday from 2:15 p.m. to 3:00 p.m. Late work policy Full text of the book we're reading Study guide Discussion questions	
Class: Writing for College, period 3	
For the week of: April 6–April 10	
Attendance questions: Monday: None Tuesday: What's the best thing about living in Wisconsin? Wednesday: What course would you like to see added to the school? Thursday: What is the best book or short story you've ever had to read? Friday: What is something good that happened this week?	
Weekly learning targets: "Produce clear and coherent writing in which the development, organization, and style are appropriate to task, purpose, and audience."	
Monday, April 6	No school
Tuesday, April 7	Recording Introduction Complete survey Journal: If you had another hour in a day, how would you spend it? Email tutorial: Thank-you letter due on LMS at start of class tomorrow
Wednesday, April 8	Recording Complete survey Journal: If you were in charge, what would you immediately change? Discuss and set schedule for roundtable Read chapter 1
Thursday, April 9	Recording Quiz Journal: If you found an animal in the street, what would you do? Discuss chapter 1 Read chapter 2
Friday, April 10	Recording Quiz Journal: Write a note to a teacher who inspired you, saying how you have used what they taught you in your life currently. Discuss chapter 2 Read chapter 3

Source for standard: National Governors Association Center for Best Practices & Council of Chief State School Officers, 2010.
Source: Linnihan, 2022, p. 60.

FIGURE 2.2: An example weekly agenda.

*Visit **go.SolutionTree.com/teacherefficacy** for a free reproducible version of this figure.*

Sending Communications

Now, consider email. If you have more than one parent or guardian communication regarding the same issue—Did everyone do poorly on a recent assessment in the same general way? Is there a field trip coming up?—you may be able to send one communication that covers the general ground for the entire group.

Now consider how many incoming queries you can anticipate by sending a weekly communication ahead of time. Whether you communicate by email or a service such as Remind (www.remind.com), an ounce of prevention can go a long way. For example, consider sending a message at the year's start about grade expectations. I teach an AP Language and Composition class, so it is common for students to perform nearly a full letter grade lower than usual after the first summative assessment. I fully expect this, as it is a college-level class; students are just beginning to learn the material. Before I began communicating this in emails to families at the term's start, I regularly received alarmed family emails about their children "failing" the class. Since communicating early on about the issue, I rarely receive such messages. Families realize that their children are not alone, are not off track, and are moving in the right direction.

Save yourself *and* families time by maximizing your email communication with these actions.

- Send a weekly message update with as much detail as possible about the week ahead, anticipating a family's concerns.
- Schedule messages to be sent at a consistent time each week so families can anticipate and prioritize reading them.
- Save group messages as boilerplate text in a document so you can tweak and reuse the text for future classes. Create one document with all the messages organized by date. With the newest messages always at the top of the document, all you need to do is send the same link each week. By updating the Google Doc each week, families will always have the most updated information for your classroom.

Another way to address family emails in advance and preserve time is to provide families with knowledge through videos. I cover this topic extensively in *Capturing the Classroom: Creating Videos to Reach Students Anytime* (Linnihan, 2022). If students have an upcoming assessment that requires detailed instruction, creating a tutorial and sharing it with both students and families can get everyone on the right track. When you take a step to anticipate and resolve questions ahead of time, it will pay off for you exponentially in saving your time (and parents' and guardians' time as well). Visit www.youtube.com/watch?v=wiwcDXpmn_E for an example tutorial.

Housekeeping

For those times when sitting at your computer is not a good fit for monitoring student work, it's important to have some physical low concentration mode tasks ready. Maybe you're tidying up prior to an open house or scheduled observation, or maybe it's simply time to wrangle the supplies and paper scraps; in such cases, using low concentration mode time to take care of physical tasks is a great fit.

One way to take the reins of a naturally high-energy group activity is to play music that models the mood or vibe you want to set. Try soft pop music with lyrics that students enjoy. Not only does this create an atmosphere conducive to learning for the task at hand, but it can even improve the learning itself. Research finds that:

> when students access more than one sensory system when engaging with new information—a process often called "multimodal learning"—they learn the materials more thoroughly. Linking related music or songs to a primarily visual task, in other words, enhances learning by adding a rich auditory channel. (Gonser, 2020)

This method of learning has two applications: (1) listening to content while doing something manual and mindless, and (2) listening to music while learning content. Both conditions can lead to better memory retention.

Similarly, music can also evoke strong feelings and memories. Not only does music enhance memory, but it can make the learning environment more welcoming since it impacts the "culture of a school for the better—sparking impromptu conversations among peers and between students and teachers, for example, or providing a calming respite from the stress of a packed school day" (Gonser, 2020).

Bring on the Beethoven! The most important playlist you ever create may be the one you play at work for your students. Music has the power to ignite memories and solidify them in young learners' brains. Take advantage of the extra teaching help by choosing music that will boost your students' memories. Studies find that classical music improves performance on some cognitive and memory tasks (Mautner, 2022).

And you don't have to do it all by yourself, either. If students have the wiggles, this functions as a brain break. Although testing and purging dried-out whiteboard markers may seem like a chore to you, there is probably an eager student willing to do it for you. Look around the room and consider what students could do. As long as they are still moving steadily toward the classroom goal you determined in chapter 1 (page 7), taking small breaks for other tasks can help reset focus and take care of housekeeping at the same time. In addition to the brain break and the tidying, there are other benefits to this task: "Children in tidy classrooms tend to be happier than those in messy ones. However, when students are the ones largely creating the mess, they ought to be the ones to clean it up" (HundrED, 2017). A clean classroom (which isn't necessarily the same as a tidy room) also reduces germs (which impacts student attendance; Cox, 2019).

Of course, students take responsibility for their own personal messes, but sometimes there are more general housekeeping needs. Whether you are doing these tasks yourself or allowing students to pitch in, low concentration mode can be a great opportunity to make some improvements that don't require you to stay after work or come in on the weekend. For example, several of my students hung fairy lights around my classroom, and they are one of my favorite things.

Reflection Questions

Consider the following questions as you apply this information to your work.

- Reflect on the types of assessments you have used in your classroom most recently. Was there any crossover in the feedback you provided to individuals that could have benefited the entire class? What could you convert to group feedback to save time?
- Have you responded more than once to a similar question from a parent or guardian? How could you communicate more effectively to address these questions up front? Could you anticipate these same types of questions for a future unit and create a document or video to share in advance?
- Have you lost something that you had to spend time looking for—a file, a test, a lesson plan? What could you do to organize your files to prevent that?

CHAPTER 3
MEDIUM CONCENTRATION MODE

Medium concentration mode is the meat of the minutes (or the cream in the cookie, if you prefer). It may be relatively calm, especially compared to low concentration mode. Medium concentration mode means students may be working on independent work that requires very little supervision for periods of fifteen minutes or more. In this mode, there may be minor distractions to your attention, but for the most part, consider them opportunities for quick brain bursts of activity.

When students are in medium concentration mode, it's important to shift your own work into medium concentration mode as well. Don't waste these minutes doing low concentration tasks. That is not the most efficient use of these minutes, which are more valuable.

One way to hold yourself accountable for how you spend time is by keeping a basic time log of what you do on the clock. This is a temporary task so you build a picture or understanding about where your time goes; don't continue filling in the log for more than a few weeks (and they have to be typical days—no assemblies or fire drills, for instance). A simple notebook or the reproducible "Daily Log" (page 55) on the edge of your desk might be enough of a visual reminder to keep a running log. Create a column each for low, medium, and high concentration tasks. If you are unsure of which column is correct, you can always review it later and shift the task to a different column. When you look back at what you recorded and see inefficient patterns, consider what was happening at the time. Where can you make more of your minutes? Sometimes, the gaps that we neglect to record are the most telling of all! Resist the temptation to analyze the minutes as you go through the day; just keep it simple by writing them down. Before you start, you might visit https://tinyurl.com/56pvx9xd to try a time management quiz.

Read on for medium concentration mode activities for students and teachers.

Medium Concentration Mode Activities for Students

The sweet spot for learning time for students depends on their ages. Elementary schoolers are more focused in the mornings (Klein, 2020); adolescents aren't that far off from that, with their learning being best during mid-morning (Dikker et al., 2020). Flexibility is key if you teach secondary students, since you may have the same class at 8:00 a.m. and again at 2:00 p.m.

Examples of medium concentration mode activities for students follow.

- **Self-guided reading or writing:** If you have meaningful reading or writing activities for your students to complete, medium concentration mode is a great time to have them do it. Instead of assigning these tasks as homework, complete some of your own medium mode tasks while they read or write. This way, you are available if students need assistance. If homework compliance is an issue, providing focused time in class can move students toward the goal.

- **Watching ten- to fifteen-minute educational or entertaining videos:** Students may be watching a short documentary piece for a social studies class or a TED-Ed speaker for art. Because you have selected the video, you know exactly how long it will take and can perfectly pair your own tasks to maximize your time.

- **Watching short instructional or tutorial videos:** One advantage of generating a well-planned video tutorial for students is that you can rest assured your message is consistent and complete every time you share it with a class. For example, a video about a particular step in a research paper or steps students need to take during a lab is a video you can reuse in the future. Videos can also be helpful if students are absent or need more repetition to grasp a concept, and recording the instructions and making them available to access anytime helps them and you.

- **Doing student-led small-group work:** Depending on your students' maturity levels, providing opportunities for them to work in student-led small-group work can help build community, autonomy (Ferlazzo, 2021), and, coincidentally, more medium concentration mode time for you as well.

The following sections provide some further ideas for when students are working on projects and so on.

Be careful not to sabotage your time by creating activities to give yourself fifteen minutes of medium concentration mode time. It's like using a credit card to pay for something because you don't have the money to purchase it. If you don't have the time now, you are unlikely to have it later. Buying fifteen minutes of working time now packs a big punch if you end up having to grade the product, costing you upward of an hour. That's a terrible interest rate! Consider activities that result in students immediately sharing with peers or small groups instead.

Watching Short Instructional or Tutorial Videos

One of my greatest hacks in the classroom is a perfect fit for your medium concentration mode tasks. Recorded tutorials that you create for students offer many possibilities. Although it takes time up front to record videos, the time they save in the long run is worthwhile, as you are heading off numerous email queries from families or trying to repeatedly reteach lessons.

You can record during quiet prep time (a high concentration mode task) or, occasionally, at home. While I don't normally advocate taking work home, the videos generally do not exceed five minutes. If I had used my teacher time wisely at work, I would have already planned the video's content. That makes the actual recording a minimal time investment. Remember, the recordings do not need to be perfect. If a bell or announcement sounds during the recording, just pause in your delivery as you would when teaching a live class.

Consider the following upsides for students:

- Adjust instruction speed to fit individual need
- Get more equitable access for attention deficit hyperactivity disorder and autism
- Access interactive study tools
- Review content and prepare for assessments
- Access material missed due to absence
- Be included if homebound or requiring extended absence
- Improve public speaking and communication skills
- Bolster remote teaching and learning (Linnihan, 2022, p. 6)

With these benefits in mind, and in light of whether your students are capable of watching such videos without assistance, consider what uses you and your students and their families might have for videos that you can create. Here is a short list.

- **Lectures:** Any lecture worth repeating is worth recording. Whether you are going to play a recording during class or only make it available online for students to access on their own after live instruction, having a recording is a nice backup. If you are unexpectedly absent, the classroom does not need to come to a screeching halt. Students can still get instruction *from you* as you had originally planned. If you are using the recording while present in the classroom, you have just duplicated yourself, freeing yourself to complete medium concentration mode tasks while students listen to virtual you.

- **Whole-class discussions or reviews:** A recording of a review is an excellent resource. Sometimes, students are absent on a review day. Other students may benefit from watching a review again. Making the video accessible to student support networks could also increase help for students at home. When a parent or guardian can access your classroom review, they can be even more helpful to their child in preparation for the upcoming assessment.

- **Assignment instructions:** Clear, concise, and consistent messaging is the gold standard for any classroom. If you record exactly what you want students to do for an assignment, students and their families can access these directions anytime. Even if you roll out the directions in person in the classroom, a recording ensures that every student has unlimited access if they have questions. If you teach the same unit in the future, you can refer back to your video to jog your memory.

- **Instructions for extensions:** Videos allow differentiation by providing enrichment or further scaffolding for students. Another unintended potential benefit is the reassurance students may feel when they know other students need the same scaffolding.

For example, you know that sometimes even the best-laid plans fall short. This often happens when I plan to return essays. I find myself racing the clock to complete the last one or two before class begins. If I have made a video that gives general feedback to the class as a whole, I can provide the feedback they all need before returning their essays. The time margin I gain is priceless, as it gives me the time I need to complete the remaining essays. You may decide to flip the order of the class period. For example, if you had planned to read a chapter of a novel after returning the essay, you can reverse that order. Playing a video of someone (me or someone else) reading the chapter for fifteen minutes often provides the necessary time I need to finish grading the last essay or two. When a student is reading along in a text, it does not matter if the reading is live or recorded, but being able to show the video does have a significant effect on my time.

Another way to cheat time with videos is by creating tutorials. They also naturally create a perfect medium concentration mode classroom environment. Essentially, students may be working on an extended project, such as a lab and report. Throughout the process, they will inevitably take the steps at a personalized pace—some will race ahead while others will need more time, possibly indicating a need for more support at various points along the way.

Creating tutorials for common sticky spots smooths the path for both you and the student. (For many of my students, it's formatting a hanging indent on a works cited page; visit www.youtube.com/watch?v=0aCDbVzANEs to see my tutorial for that as an example.) Maybe your class is working on a lab, and, in the past, you've gotten a lot of questions about step 2 of the setup process. Instead of individually reteaching five students how to do the step, in preparation, you can make tutorial videos available when they need them. For a unit with a general sequence and multiple tutorials, consider recording a tutorial for each step, embedding them into a document, and sharing the document on the classroom platform with hyperlinks to the step tutorials.

While students are watching a prerecorded video, you gain that time back in your classroom. You have the advantage of knowing exactly how long the video runs, and you can plan accordingly. To learn more, check out *Capturing the Classroom* (Linnihan, 2022).

Make sure you get your administrator's and families' permission before making any classroom recordings, since you'll be sharing the videos with students. Visit **go.SolutionTree.com/teacher efficacy** and download the free reproducible "Video Recording Permission Form" to send to families to sign if your administrator agrees that it is sufficient.

Participating in Student-Led Small-Group Work

Consider the following from the Harvard Kennedy School (n.d.) for cultivating student time in medium concentration mode. Many of these are strategies you probably already use in the classroom. The following section explores just some of these.

- **Jigsaw:** This method of piecing information together is a technique that "effectively produces academic gains in problem solving and analyzing, two important cognitive skills" (Tom, 2023). It is a perfect activity for medium concentration mode time, as it fosters student connections organically, with little to no direction from the teacher.
- **Turn-and-talk:** This method of boosting student engagement is a great way to involve students who may be hesitant to contribute to a larger group. It's easy to assign groups or partners by classroom location or proficiency levels to collectively address a topic.
- **Think-pair-share:** Taking the turn-and-talk to the next level, think-pair-share progressively moves from individual to small group to larger group sharing. After consulting with a peer, the pair prepares to share with the group as one voice. Although every student participates in the turn-and-talk discussion, the small group can select a speaker for the group to share ideas with the class.
- **Pro-con-caveat grids:** Just like the standard pro-con lists, students can team up to create a list on an assigned topic. This activity is a great springboard for any type of assignment in which students ultimately take a position on a topic. After creating a small-group list, students can rotate and merge with other groups, comparing and modifying their own lists after nuanced discussions of the items (Millis, 2014).
- **Three-step interview:** Student pairs interview each other, then combine with another pair to share what they learned (Davidson, Major, & Michaelsen, 2014; Harvard Kennedy School, n.d).

The jigsaw format I discuss here provides two separate medium concentration mode opportunities for the teacher: (1) during the initial small group discussion time, when students need little to no supervision, and (2) during any subject's writing time.

1. Create groups. Depending on what they're doing, homogenous or heterogenous groups might work best. If you're using random groups, consider using Picker Wheel (https://pickerwheel.com/tools/random-team-generator), which shoots confetti when it reveals the teams.
2. Assign a different discussion question related to the day's assignment to each team. The team takes notes, shares ideas, and formulates a group answer to share with the rest of the class.
3. After an appropriate amount of time (usually between ten and fifteen minutes), each group takes a turn sharing their ideas with the whole class.
4. While each group presents, the rest of the class takes notes on each question analysis throughout the discussion in anticipation of forming their own responses to the question.

This is an excellent way to move quickly through prompts, giving an in-depth look at each one, but saving time by having various groups analyze only one specific question. After each group shares its response, you can use a random number generator to select one of the questions the entire class will use as an extended response prompt (which works well in many subject areas). Students can do a deep dive into one particular issue, such as historical events in a social studies class, composers in a music class, or various classifications of elements and their properties in a science class. Try it with a long article that you want the entire class to read; assign sections of it to small groups, then have them present their section to the class while everyone else takes notes. Rather than having the full class read a ten-page article, everyone can benefit and learn in this focused and condensed workload distribution.

You might follow up the activity with a quick-write on one of the student-led shares. Of course, the students whose own question is selected feel like they have won the lottery. Randomize the groups each day for balance. Consider allowing students to use their notes. They learn that it benefits them to pay attention to the other groups' answers, as it may help them on the upcoming writing task. Students are invested in the discussion and generally produce better writing than if they had worked entirely alone.

The good news is that this type of instruction is *beneficial* for students, since:

> small-group learning (when compared to competitive and individualistic learning) improves academic achievement, relationships with classmates and faculty, and promotes psychological well-being . . . students are better at solving problems and develop a deeper understanding of the material when working in groups. Regardless of subject, students learn more and retain material longer in small-group learning than when the same content is presented in other instructional practices. Attendance, efficiency, and persistence improve. (Harvard Kennedy School, n.d., pp. 1, 2)

If the necessary grading that this produces still feels like too much additional work, consider having the group present the answer to the class by using a slide instead of culminating with a writing assignment.

Medium Concentration Mode Tasks for Teachers

As a mother of four children, many time-management skills I use were born out of necessity. Some wise person once told me to sleep when the baby sleeps. As hard as it was to take that advice instead of getting something done (cramming down a sandwich, taking a bathroom break, showering, cleaning the house) during naptime, the advice was valid. Although I don't advise napping at work, the philosophy of *matching the mode* rings true in the classroom. Take advantage of the relative calm and quiet when students are in this mode to do your own medium concentration mode tasks. It's an investment in your well-rested sanity!

As mentioned, during medium concentration mode, students may be working independently or in small groups, needing little to no guidance. You can comfortably concentrate here, although whenever students are present, there is an inherent responsibility to monitor behaviors. Your productivity with tasks requiring this deeper concentration will be manageable in ten- to fifteen-minute chunks of time.

Have this work ready to go when the time arrives. Tasks such as grading or writing—those that take up your after-work hours—often fall into this category. If you are interrupted mid-task, it will likely be brief. It should be fairly easy to jump right back into your work.

Examples of medium concentration mode activities for teachers follow.

- Providing verbal feedback for small groups or one-to-one
- Drafting emails
- Grading brief writings (portions of lab reports, response writings, explanations for computations)
- Assessing student worksheets that require comprehension analysis
- Planning for the next high concentration mode

The following sections provide some further ideas for teachers to take on when students are in medium concentration mode.

> Planning what *not* to do can be as important as planning what *to do* with your time. Short windows of time may seem insignificant, so the temptation can be to waste them on tasks that are either the wrong mode or simply distractions. Establishing rules for yourself helps you stay on track. For example, turning off notifications on your computer, phone, smartwatch, or iPad (anything that shouts, "Look at me") while at work will help keep you focused. Close your browser to webpages that have the potential to lure you down a rabbit hole, and set specific times to check email. If you are worried about missing something important, changing settings to allow certain people to penetrate your bubble is easy.

Providing Verbal Feedback for Small Groups or One-to-One

Some medium concentration mode teacher tasks have the potential to take the place of longer, more time-consuming styles of providing feedback. When you have a giant stack of papers to grade, don't feel you must commit to grading the whole stack. Being able to assess is something that goes faster if you're an experienced teacher (and if you're an inexperienced teacher, you will learn). It's *documenting* the feedback that is time consuming.

If you can assess what a student needs to work on quickly when looking at an assignment or assessment, consider speaking one-to-one with the student to provide personal feedback for a few minutes rather than doing it in writing. Immediacy affects feedback's effectiveness. Educator Rachel Goddard (2023) states:

> Verbal feedback is effective because it is often given during, or very quickly following, the learning or task. It offers more opportunity for dialogue between you and your pupil, ensuring that they understand the feedback, enabling them to respond to it and to action the feedback straight away.

Explain to students ahead of time that they need to take notes during your discussion so they can refer back to them as they go forward, revise, or try again. This note-taking boosts student autonomy, which provides a host of benefits (Núñez & León, 2015; Okada, 2021), and writing information by hand provides improved recall (Umejima, Ibaraki, Yamazaki, & Sakai, 2021).

You may have a tendency to fantasize about the perfect working conditions to "get it all done." Many teachers sacrifice their days off to do exactly this. Not only is that harmful to your body, soul, and relationships, but it probably is not the best way to knock it all out.

The average adult attention span is twenty minutes (Cooper & Richards, 2016). Taking frequent pauses (whether we have control or not, such as in the classroom) may be the most productive way to manage our time, since breaks:

> can improve well-being and also help with getting more work done. Counter to the popular narrative of working long work hours, our research suggests that taking breaks within work hours not only does not detract from performance, but can help boost it. (Lyubykh & Gulseren, 2023)

This will require a shift in mindset around how one works. Recognize that shifting gears without having completed any one task does not mean a hit to productivity.

Drafting Emails for Future Send

One of the best technological advancements of the modern era is the message scheduling tool. During medium concentration mode, I often work on communications to send in the future. By working in draft mode, I can easily return to the message if I get interrupted and need to step away from it. This type of mode is often a "just right" fit for knocking out a task like this, but if it falls short, it's easy to jump right back into it if the message is saved as a draft.

Having boilerplate text for similar kinds of emails that you have to send will help ease this task. Do you send many messages similar to the following?

- Reminders
- Weekly parent updates
- Schedule changes
- Event notifications
- Seasonal event or project directions

One benefit to scheduling communications in *draft* mode is that you can add to or revise a message before sending it. If you have a last-minute update to add, you can easily do so. As a parent of four children, I found the number of emails overwhelming when they were all in school. One simple way to control your messaging and ensure that everyone has received and can return to important information is to create a Google Doc that contains the email text you sent to the group in one place. That way, if families miss a communication, they can easily scan that document to find what they missed. Your communication each time may be as simple as "Here is the essential information document link." This frees you to update, add, and revise at any time.

Grading Brief Writings

There was a time in my career when I looked forward to sitting down to a stack of tests and grading them from top to bottom without interruption. Now, I realize that grading this way is impractical. Breaking down my grading into sections can improve my practice. Shifting gears and taking breaks are key to functioning as a productive adult. Sprinting through a grading session would be exhausting and inefficient. Give your brain and body the grace to take necessary breaks so you are focused and ready when you return to the task. Taking breaks, as mentioned in assistant professors Zhanna Lyubykh and Duygu Biricik Gulseren's (2023) commentary about work research, is both necessary and productive. When you finish your chunk of mode, stretch, take a few deep breaths, or refill your water bottle. You might even try a one-minute plank to realign your spine after sitting.

Unlike grading multiple choice assessments or sections, short responses require a higher level of concentration to evaluate, but they don't necessarily need a large block of time to score. Grading multiple choice is much easier to do with low-level distractions that are more likely to occur in low concentration mode. And if the short writings are part of a large project or assessment, it's OK to take medium mode moments to grade only those pieces. Grading a full set of tests one page at a time means not immediately knowing how each student did, but it may take less time than assessing each test individually from start to finish. Grading every student's response to the same prompt consecutively can make it easier to focus and compare subtle differences between answers.

Planning for the Next High Concentration Mode

Just as it is important to have a to-do list for the kickoff of low concentration mode minutes, it is also important to make a plan for working in the other modes. The best time to do this planning is during medium concentration mode, as this ensures the opportunities to chip away at this important work don't fall between the cracks, costing you more time later. The following quote tends to apply to high concentration mode tasks:

We can put off tasks when they seem dauntingly large. "Prep year 6 history" can feel like a big undertaking. But you can try breaking it down into smaller steps. Tackle them one at a time, and enjoy the feeling of satisfaction when you tick each one off. Don't forget to update your list regularly to keep you on top of your tasks. (Education Support, n.d.)

Taking time to plan—a medium concentration mode task—at the start of high concentration mode is a waste of your valuable time. At the secondary school level, teacher planning time each day is different depending on schedules. The adjustment to a new term can be brutal if you are used to planning at the start of the day, and suddenly, your prep time is the last hour before you leave—especially if you are more productive at the start of the day (or vice versa).

One comment I frequently hear from those who like to plan at the end of the day is that they are so exhausted by the time their prep rolls around that they waste half of it just trying to figure out what to do next. A plan makes all the difference! Medium concentration mode is a great time to jot down a list of tasks to do during your next high concentration mode, which is the focus of the next chapter.

Reflection Questions

Consider the following questions as you apply this information to your work.

- How do you currently manage your time? After tracking for a few days, how accurate was your assessment of your own time? Were you surprised by the results? How does this insight affect how you will manage your future time?
- Consider logging the questions from students and families over a few days, tallying similar ones that are repeated. Are there any questions that you could address in a short video for future use?
- Consider content you have taught recently (or anticipate for the future). Is there dense information that would work well as a jigsaw activity for students to present to each other?
- Are there ways you can generate additional medium concentration mode time in your classroom?

Daily Log

For three typical days (and no more than five), record your time. Record tasks in no longer than fifteen-minute increments (and less if you notice).

Date	
From (Time)	Action

Date	
From (Time)	Action

Date	
From (Time)	Action

Teacher Time Management © 2025 Solution Tree Press • SolutionTree.com
Visit **go.SolutionTree.com/teacherefficacy** to download this free reproducible.

CHAPTER 4
HIGH CONCENTRATION MODE

There are good reasons that some employers offer overtime and holiday bonus pay. It is inherently more valuable time than the standard workday. Although educators do not often receive this type of compensation unless they are taking on an overloaded schedule, I recommend looking at prep time in a similar manner. Typically, time spent in preparation or planning is the contractual time during the work day that teachers have to make discretionary decisions about their time. That being said, many districts require professional development, meetings, co-worker coverage, and co-planning demands on this time. The remainder of the minutes may feel like they are barely existent at times, so making the most of them is more important than ever. The times you get to *choose* what you are doing and how you do it are invaluable. Whether this happens every day for a predictable duration or just once a week, it's important to recognize its value and maximize its potential.

While the low and medium modes limit your ability to concentrate and how much time you have to complete a task, the most significant limitation for high concentration mode is its scarcity. Recognizing when you are in this mode is critical. You want to have a solid plan ready and hit the ground running. Low and medium modes are slower, but you may relate to Tom Cruise's *Top Gun* character Maverick, who famously declares, "I feel the need, the need for speed" (Scott, 1986).

The second limitation of this mode is the discipline it takes to remain focused on a task that requires significant concentration. Although you may find yourself frequently lamenting the lack of time you have to grade written assessments or plan units, it's easy to waste opportunities to do this type of intense work because more enjoyable tasks are available. Students have the same temptations to shift gears into other modes. It may be perfectly quiet in the classroom, but as you know, that does not necessarily mean students are working on the appropriate task. Some monitoring is necessary to move everyone toward the goal. Providing reminders and teaching students to recognize when they are in high concentration mode will build their time-management skills.

Read on for high concentration mode activities for students and teachers.

High Concentration Mode Activities for Students

High concentration mode activities for students require focus and discipline. The atmosphere during this mode is likely quiet and deeply conducive to learning. (This allows you to work on intense tasks simultaneously.) It's important to acknowledge when students are working productively in this mode and encourage them to continue the habit. Research supports "acknowledging or giving approval for correct responding and appropriate behavior. Praise has been shown to be an effective reinforcer when it is specific, meaning it describes what the individual has done well" (Ennis, Royer, Lane, & Dunlap, 2020). Verbalize your appreciation at the conclusion of a task to commend them on their focused, hard work (and consider sending home a note or email acknowledging their focus). Of course, every class has its own mix of students and dynamics, depending on abilities and maturity levels, but as Brookfield Central High School principal Brett Gruetzmacher tells the students every day during announcements, "Scan the world for the positive and never miss a chance to say thank you" (personal communication, September 3, 2024). Praise is free, so give it freely!

It's important to match the minutes with students. If they are in high concentration mode, you have the same opportunity to be just as focused as they are.

Examples of high concentration mode activities for students follow. Note that each task should be a minimum of fifteen minutes.

High Concentration Mode

- Sustained reading
- Peer editing and proofing (read the Peer-Guided Feedback section, page 15, for more on this topic)
- Watching and responding to a read-aloud or podcast
- Creating student projects
- Researching or note-taking

The following sections provide some further ideas.

Sustained Silent Reading

Sustained silent reading (SSR) is a time when students (and maybe even teachers) grab something to read for enjoyment, usually for somewhere between ten to thirty minutes. While students have assigned reading in various classes or topics, the selection for this time should be outside that scope. The sole purpose of this time is to foster positive reading habits and curiosity (Gamber-Thompson, 2019).

Some people erroneously believe that reading belongs in the English language arts classroom. I tutor young people for standardized tests such as the ACT and SAT, so I find it interesting when someone concludes that the science sections of those tests are *reading* tests. Of course, they are! Students in all grades benefit from "discipline-specific strategies" for reading (Gazith, 2024, p. 99).

 Sustained silent reading, especially in content areas that include much academic vocabulary, works only for students who are proficient readers. Therefore, the concept of sustained silent reading comes with the caveat that students who are not proficient readers should not spend unattended classroom time doing this (Hasbrouck, 2006). Preteaching *academic vocabulary* (words that are specific to content areas such as science and history) is also required (Ortlieb & Cheek, 2013) and is especially helpful for English learners (Calderón & Slakk, 2018).

Having a purpose when reading a text is an important part of sustained reading (Gazith, 2024). For example, after preteaching the required academic vocabulary used in an upcoming article for U.S. history and providing the necessary context, students can use the plus, minus, interesting strategy (de Bono, 1995). The strategy, a completed example of which is in figure 4.1 (page 60), engages students in what they have read in a way that requires high concentration. (Again, this assumes all students in the class are proficient readers; if not, this isn't an appropriate exercise.)

> Text from a Franklin D. Roosevelt speech, March 12, 1933:
>
> This is a day of national consecration. And I am certain that on this day my fellow Americans expect that on my induction into the Presidency I will address them with a candor and a decision which the present situation of our people impels. This is preeminently the time to speak the truth, the whole truth, frankly and boldly. Nor need we shrink from honestly facing conditions in our country today. This great Nation will endure as it has endured, will revive and will prosper. So, first of all, let me assert my firm belief that the only thing we have to fear is fear itself—nameless, unreasoning, unjustified terror which paralyzes needed efforts to convert retreat into advance. In every dark hour of our national life a leadership of frankness and vigor has met with that understanding and support of the people themselves which is essential to victory. I am convinced that you will again give that support to leadership in these critical days. (Roosevelt, 1933)
>
> | | |
> |---|---|
> | **P: plus (or positive)** | That he is addressing the people with honesty |
> | **M: minus (or negative)** | That the country is in a bad situation |
> | **I: interesting** | That he says the only thing you have to fear is fear itself |

Source: Gazith, 2024, p. 106.

FIGURE 4.1: Plus, minus, interesting strategy example.

> I am a huge believer in incentives. Finding out what students value and a matching task can have tremendous returns. For example, you may reward a high-performing class with time spent on what they value (watching a funny video short or taking an outdoor break) for full success in a particular goal. Perhaps you have an honors English language arts class where students have a semester term paper due. If 90 percent of students complete it on time, you may spend time coaxing the remaining 10 percent to the finish line. Instead, look into communicating with students and families, having one-to-one conferencing with the students, or reteaching those concepts. If all students turn in their papers on time, however, you might have a bit more high concentration mode time.

Watching and Responding to a Read-Aloud, Video, or Podcast

As mentioned previously, using someone (or something) other than you to engage students in content can have tremendous benefits—not the least of which is its ability to generate more time for you. Assigning a video paired with a comprehension exercise, such as a worksheet or reflection, can naturally place the students in high concentration mode, giving you some solid high concentration mode time, too. These may include read-alouds by proficient students or recordings of yourself doing the reading, or videos or audio you or others have created (such as a biopic or documentary, TEDTalk, or a podcast). Asking students to complete an accompanying plus, minus, interesting form like that in figure 4.1 can increase "critical thinking and decision-making skills" and make "classroom interaction effective" (Sharma & Saarsar, 2017, p. 974).

Creating Projects

Research shows that students benefit from increased autonomy to be creative in school (McCombs, 2015). Your students may want to see past examples of ways they can model their work. This reinforces that we need to push creative boundaries and provide more opportunities for students to take chances with their work. Research backs this effort since "Teachers who practice creativity in learning and use technology in transformative ways are most likely to see positive student outcomes" (Gallup, 2019, p. 19).

Generally, once students develop an idea and strategy, their creative projects are the ones that they enjoy the most. Creating videos is an excellent way for students of all ages to showcase their knowledge and utilize technology to make delivery more engaging to the class. While recording can require some flexibility in location (possibly in the hallway), the planning time is perfect for high concentration mode. Students may be designing in a creative program such as Canva or creating video content in a platform that allows students to record and edit such as iMovie.

High Concentration Mode Activities for Teachers

If there is one guiding principle that I use when considering how to plan to use my high concentration mode minutes, it is this: *Is there something or someone else that I can copy to multiply my minutes?* I don't mean plagiarism; I mean genuine sharing. Is there a resource I can modify to maximize my prep time? I need to ask myself if what I am doing right now has ever been done before by someone else. If the answer is *yes*, then why am I attempting to reinvent the wheel while I spin my own wheels? Am I assessing something that someone else has assessed before? Then, I should be using and modifying that rubric rather than starting from scratch.

Just because we want more of this time does not mean it is comfortable or pleasant. It is challenging and demanding. The self-discipline required to do these tasks whenever that kind of time is available is significant. Finding success with your high concentration tasks is directly connected to good time management (Csapai, Varga, & Berke, 2020). Prioritizing tasks and the delayed gratification of knowing you will be able to enjoy more downtime at home if you complete these tasks, even when difficult, will make a difference.

When it comes to managing time well, we all have our tendencies and proclivities. Mine include my freakish devotion to morning workouts. We also all have our own chronotype, or *diurnal preference*, which dictates when our bodies like to wake and sleep (Kalmbach et al., 2017). Despite what your feelings are about getting up early when it's dark outside, consider this from over thirty years of research on successful people:

> Most people can engage in deliberate practice—which means pushing oneself beyond current limits—for only an hour without rest . . . and that many experts prefer to begin training early in the morning when mental and physical energy is readily available. (Ericsson, 2006, as cited in Jabr, 2013)

So, take advantage of early morning hours if you can, and make sure you don't stay in high concentration mode for more than an hour (which, of course, will rarely, if ever, happen at school).

Examples of high concentration mode activities for teachers follow.

- Creating assessments
- Grading assessments
- Working on professional advancement such as coursework, grant proposals, and self-reflection
- Writing letters of recommendation

The following sections provide details about these ideas.

Grading, planning, creating, sending communications, and other seemingly benign and easy-to-knock-out tasks are tempting to do at home when you may have more control over your time and can limit your distractions. Occasionally, I take work home. Some tasks take time but require very little focus, so I can easily do them while watching TV or relaxing outside. Just be careful to set boundaries for your mental and physical health. Setting realistic limits about what you do outside of the workday is necessary for balance. Fight the temptation to regularly do schoolwork at home—especially if it is pulling you away from your important relationships (including the one with yourself).

Creating Assessments

In my first years of teaching, creating assessments and materials was an overwhelming time suck. I created study guides for Shakespeare plays, typing them out the night before we read each act. Although I am grateful that I invested that time, I am painfully aware that my students could have used perfectly good resources that already existed. Don't go it alone. Collaborate with colleagues, tap into online resources, try generative AI, and detail your rubrics.

COLLABORATE WITH COLLEAGUES

Take advantage of collaborative planning with colleagues. Planning "opens up mental space and . . . distribute[s] the workload" (DeLussey, n.d.). When you produce great work, share it. Common formative assessments, a mainstay in professional learning communities, result from a group of teachers who teach the same topic or grade level taking the following steps around their tests and quizzes (Bailey & Jakicic, 2023).

1. Decide what to assess.
2. Decide how to assess.
3. Develop the assessment plan.
4. Determine the timeline.
5. Write the assessment.
6. Review the assessment before administration.
7. Set proficiency criteria and decide how to gather the data.

As a guide for those unfamiliar with collaborative teacher teams, figure 4.2 (page 64) offers a checklist.

Design	Yes	No
The targets come from identified power or essential standards.		
The assessment is written around learning targets, not standards.		
The assessment is written around a small number of learning targets.		
The purpose is to provide time and support rather than a grade.		
The type of assessment item the team uses matches the learning target's level of thinking.		
The team writes the selected-response items to find out what students know, not to trick them.		
Constructed-response items provide context and specific directions to make expectations clear to students.		
The team agrees on what proficiency looks like for each target.		
The team creates an answer guide for its assessment.		
Use		
The team collaboratively writes and administers the assessment in a common way.		
The team collaboratively scores items using a common rubric.		
The data meeting happens as quickly as possible after the assessment.		
All teachers bring their data, including student work, to the data meeting for discussion.		
The teachers use data for planning what to do next, not to judge their effectiveness.		
Students are involved; they know the learning targets and receive feedback on their work.		
Students get more time and support based on the results.		
Teachers reassess students after corrective instruction.		
Students who master learning targets receive more challenging work after teachers analyze the data.		

Source: Bailey & Jakicic, 2023, p. 81.

FIGURE 4.2: Common formative assessments checklist.

Visit **go.SolutionTree.com/teacherefficacy** for a free reproducible version of this figure.

TAP INTO ONLINE RESOURCES

Online resources abound. If you're creating review materials or assessments, odds are good something exists that you can modify for your classroom use. Don't be afraid to ask students what their favorite study resources are; they might point you in the right direction. Use any online search engine for digital tools and apps teachers can use to support formative assessments. Search online for websites that offer assessments about a particular topic (or look for open-ended topics).

The Canvas (www.instructure.com/canvas) platform, a learning management system familiar to many schools, has a Commons page with materials provided by other teachers. You can import entire units or just pick and choose what you want directly into your own class page. The Commons page also allows you to upload your courses and units to keep for yourself or to share with others or with your district.

Quizlet (https://quizlet.com) is a popular review resource. The site generates electronic flashcards and other interactive games with the uploaded material. One of the beauties is that although teachers can upload and create reviews, students can—and should!—upload review materials, too. Not only do you save time by not having to create the review materials yourself, but you also have an excellent resource for students to use to create some additional high concentration mode time in the classroom. Assigning fifteen minutes of Quizlet review before the start of an assessment will extend your own high concentration mode time and may improve the performance of your students on the assessment.

TRY GENERATIVE AI

Science fiction author Ray Bradbury (as cited in Rundle, 2012) once speculated, "I don't think the robots are taking over. I think the men who play with toys have taken over. And if we don't take the toys out of their hands, we're fools." With the explosion of generative AI, such as Google's Gemini and OpenAI's ChatGPT, it may feel that humanity is about to lose a battle against technology. I tend to lean more in line with Bradbury: We are still in control, and how we put technology to work to improve our lives will be the difference. Ignoring AI will not make it disappear, so I encourage you to embrace it. You'll want to know what students are exploring. Surveys report different percentages of students using generative AI—for example, 18 percent of middle and high school students report using it (Touchstone Research, 2023) and 46 percent of tenth and eleventh graders report using it (Schiel, Bobek, & Schnieders, 2023). Learning as much as you can about the tools and what they offer will help you address their use in your classroom.

How do you put generative AI tools such as ChatGPT, Gemini, and others to work for you? You use it to generate review questions for content understanding that you know and trust. Copy and paste the text into the tool and ask it to write review questions. If those questions don't hit the mark, give it more specific directions: *develop essay prompts*, *make the questions multiple choice*, and *include more questions about World War II* are examples of how to get what you need.

You also can encourage students to use generative AI to create "review questions on a specific topic, then have them see if they can get the correct answers" (Staake, 2023). For example, English language arts teachers often have students ask for sentence examples for parts of speech. AI can create multiple examples on the spot. Students can prompt it to provide ten examples of passive voice sentences, squinting modifiers, or comma splices. This frees you up for more potential high concentration mode tasks because you're not fielding these questions. Students can benefit as well: "A 2020 study on using AI for both formative and summative assessment in a data science course showed that students using the formative assessment system for ongoing self-assessment reported **higher grades and better understanding** of analytical methods" (Vittorini, Menini, & Tonelli, 2021, as cited in European Commission, 2023; bold in original).

Formative (www.formative.com/ai-powered) is a somewhat heavily researched teacher tool. Drop your own text into it and prompt it to generate specific quiz questions based on it. The site generates questions based on the difficulty level you select and assigns point values that work for you. You can customize further by adding hints for students. Language teacher Wenjing Huang (2023) explains that "this feature greatly saves teachers time that would normally be dedicated to brainstorming how to support learners with hints." Grading assessments are another place you can save time by using generative AI since "summative teacher assessments using the automated tool [Formative] **reduced time spent and increased accuracy** compared to manual grading" (Vittorini, Menini, & Tonelli, 2021, as cited in European Commission, 2023; bold in original).

It is important to check with your administrator to make sure you know what your system's AI policies are and to check with your school's IT department. And, of course, be cautious: It's important to recognize that generative AI relies on its human users to ensure complete accuracy and check sources. Ownership of the material falls squarely on the teacher's shoulders.

If you are writing a parent communication, you can provide basic details to include and then give a specific prompt regarding tone, such as *Use a lighthearted and encouraging tone*. You can type, *Sound more professional* or *Use basic vocabulary*. The more direct, concise, and specific you are, the more likely you are to get a product that meets your expectations (Markman, 2023).

DETAIL YOUR RUBRICS

Adding detailed descriptions and criteria to your rubrics can take some time up front but may make grading easier. For example, I added details to a persuasive speech rubric (part of which is depicted in figure 4.3). That detail allows me to *highlight* rather than write out my feedback.

	Ideas and Content	Organization	Voice	Word Choice	Sentence Fluency	Conventions
4 Ten points	Clear and focused thesis that is debatable Details relevant and fully elaborated Citing at least two sources accurately and appropriately (title, author, date, publisher) (minimum two sources that are not online articles) Excellent topic	Logical order Strong introduction, body, and conclusion Effective and sophisticated use of transitions Sufficiently addresses and knocks down counter argument Builds to strongest supporting point	Strong creativity and interesting ideas Strong evidence of speaker's personality (enthusiasm and energy)	Strong, well-developed vocabulary Terminology defined effectively Appropriate for audience	All sentences complete Variety of styles and lengths Comfortable flow enhances speaking Has full command of audience	Strong sense of correct speaking conventions: • Grammar • Pause • Emphasis • Pronunciation • Articulation • Rate • Projection
3 Nine points	Clear and focused thesis Details not fully elaborated Citing some, not all, sources Good topic Did not state one or more: • Title • Author • Date • Publication	Logical order Good introduction, body, and conclusion Some use of transitions	Some creativity and interesting ideas Some evidence of speaker's personality (enthusiasm and energy) Reading from cards or SMART board affected connection with audience	Well-developed vocabulary Terminology somewhat defined effectively Appropriate for audience	Most sentences complete Some variety of styles and lengths Comfortable flow	Generally correct use of speaking conventions

FIGURE 4.3: Persuasive speech rubric with details.

continued ↓

	Ideas and Content	Organization	Voice	Word Choice	Sentence Fluency	Conventions
2 Eight points	Attempts to address thesis Details limited Minimal attempt to cite sources Read quotes, but didn't cite source Choose topic more carefully	Some sense of logical order Weak introduction, body, and conclusion Limited use of transitions	Limited creativity and interesting ideas Little evidence of speaker's personality (enthusiasm and energy)	Words correct, but not precise or vivid Somewhat appropriate for audience	Sentences need developing Little variety of styles and lengths Choppy or rambling Ending with a questioning tone	Some errors in conventions distract the listener Need to pump it up
1 Zero to seven points	No clear sense of thesis Few or no details Failed to cite any source Topic does not work well	No logical order Lacks transitions Missing intro "Did you know?" "Have you ever wondered?" Missing conclusion "That's it"	Little or no creativity No evidence of speaker's personality (enthusiasm and energy)	Words are vague or incorrect Terminology not defined Filler words (such as *like* and *um*)	Many errors in speech fluency Up-endings undermined credibility Long pauses Lost in notes Reading word for word from notes Sing-song cadence	Many errors in conventions distract the listener Pace was too rushed to demonstrate effective pauses or emphasis Couldn't hear

The key to keeping the rubric relevant and accurate is to continually tweak it. For instance, based on teaching nine-week classes on a block schedule, you might revisit assignments four times each school year. I recommend not modifying a rubric mid-unit after students have begun working on the assignment, but you also don't want to miss an opportunity to make improvements for the future. If you find yourself writing feedback on a rubric while grading, add it to your copy of the rubric so that a newer, better version will be ready to roll out in nine weeks. Similarly, if students are consistently missing an important detail or failing to include essential content—on a lab report, a musical review, or a mathematical problem explanation—adding that criteria to the rubric will prompt the next group of students to address it to the extent you seek.

Consider creating a key and marking up papers with shorthand. For example, for a lab report, missing units are something you want to draw students' attention to. You can come up with shorthand code for that issue and use it (ten times across your twenty-five-person class). Just make sure students have the key for the shorthand before you return their assessments. If students handwrite an assessment, perhaps instruct them to write on every other line of the page and to write on the front side only. This is a minor request, but it makes the final product much easier on the eyes for grading. If you grade online with a platform such as Canvas, generating comments in a bank also saves time.

Grading Assessments

Not only does assessing take significant time, but it also requires intense focus. Emotions can creep in. (How could they *miss* this? Have I taught them *anything*?) Maintaining an even demeanor and persevering can test the very fiber of one's being. The struggle does not have to take such a significant toll on us, however. There are a few options to make the mountain more manageable.

TRY GENERATIVE AI

Here, again, is an area where generative AI can help you, as it can help make assessments fully or partly automated. One machine, called c-rater-ML, is shown to "produce scores that were comparable to human raters in scoring students' responses to constructed response questions" (Liu, Rios, Heilman, Gerard, & Linn, 2016, as cited in Hopfenbeck, Zhang, Sun, Robertson, & McGrane, 2023).

This comparability between AI and human scores for written assessment responses holds true across multiple cases (Jung, Tyack, & von Davier, 2022; Wahlen et al., 2020). This also enables almost instant formative feedback, which can be pivotal to feedback's effectiveness (Brookhart, 2017).

USE OTHER ELECTRONIC GRADING TOOLS

If you have access to an electronic grading option, such as quizzes on Canvas or Gradescope (www.gradescope.com), you can eliminate the work of grading objective portions of assessments altogether. Keep these considerations in mind when taking this approach.

- **Keep tabs on students:** Check in on student assessments despite any automation. You will want to keep sight of how each student is doing in your class. Psychologically, if you are physically marking questions as incorrect, the student's performance is more likely to stick with you. It's important to really take a look at how each student did and process it.

- **Be on the alert for trends:** If you are physically grading a test, you may be more likely to notice if nearly everyone is missing a particular question. It could be a poorly written question, or your key could be incorrect. Another possibility is that you did not cover the material sufficiently prior to the assessment. Looking over the results and watching for trends will guide you on how to improve your instruction in the future if repeating the unit with another class. The benefit of using an electronic test is that if you have used it previously, you will likely have worked out the kinks and be assured that it is valid. Similarly, if you fix an error now, it will be fixed for the future, too!

ADJUST YOUR ASSESSMENTS

Just as it is important to match modes with your students, it is also important to match how much time you spend grading an assignment with its weight in your class. Take, as an example, a small formative assignment worth ten points in a category of four hundred points, making up only 2.5 percent of the total grade. If that assignment takes an hour to assess, it's time to reconsider the assignment as a whole. If it takes an excessive amount of time to grade, perhaps it is better suited as a summative assignment worth more assessment points. If not, is there a more efficient way to assess it? Does it need assessing at all? Can the assessment or feedback be simplified in any way? What value does this feedback provide?

You can start adjusting assessments if you:

> keep track of how much time you spend grading, on which assignments, and assess if you are spending your grading time wisely. You

need to be a bit ruthless to ensure that the time spent grading is worthwhile in terms of the overall content of your course, and the weight of your assignments. (Western University Centre for Teaching and Learning, n.d.)

It's easy to get caught up in details that offer negligible, if any, benefit to your overall classroom goal and the skills students are working toward.

One classroom strategy that can help in a number of content areas—history, civics, and English language arts in particular, but also science and advisory or homeroom—is the Socratic seminar. There, students discuss a text, ask questions, and respond to each other. The protocol usually requires having students follow these steps (Facing Our History and Ourselves, 2020).

1. Students read the assigned text and prepare points and questions. The teacher may assign a discussion leader who generates a few open-ended questions to begin the seminar.
2. Before they begin, the teacher reminds students of the following.
    + The "purpose of the seminar is not to debate or prove a point but to more deeply understand what the author was trying to express in the text" (Facing Our History and Ourselves, 2020).
    + They are supposed to talk with each other, not to the discussion leader or teacher.
    + They should refer to the text for evidence of their ideas.
3. The seminar occurs, with expected silences. If students get off track or have trouble, the teacher can interject. This means that your first couple of Socratic seminars may be low or medium mode concentration activities, and later seminars turn into high concentration mode times.
4. The teacher gives students time to reflect on their experience and their participation. This reflection piece is critical to improving their performance in the following seminars. Some starter questions follow.
    + Did you see others actively listening? Building on what others said? What is your evidence of these things?
    + How is the text different to you after participating in this Socratic seminar?
    + What would you do differently next time?

The students tend to be engaged in this level of voice. Assessing it can be a struggle, however. I used to track the number of comments, which caused me to focus on quantity rather than quality. I pondered the absurdity of Socrates evaluating discussions this way. Finally, after more experience, I implemented a system that had students assess each other. Rather than tallying comments, they focused on specific comments and questions that someone contributed to the discussion. This drastically cut my grading time, and I assert that students learned more as a result.

FOCUS MORE TIME ON INSTRUCTION

Better student writing means less difficult, time-consuming grading. Taking time to preteach conventions and expectations will help students focus and produce better work. Prep students in the following manner:

- Provide examples of good theses or topic sentences
- Share the grading criteria (or rubric)
- Have a syllabus policy for papers that fail mechanics (just returned)
- Teach [students] how to revise on their own, during class time
- Provide a list of 'pet peeves' and point to online explanations (Yee, n.d., pp. 1, 2)

Generative AI can provide feedback to students before submitting their work. Students can copy the rubric into a generative AI tool, copy and paste their writing into it, and query it to assess the writing using the rubric. While it may not be a perfect analysis, it is a good way for them to catch omissions and errors.

Provide students with a cheat sheet of reminders to use during their assessment. For example, if they have a reminder directly in front of them to include units for each equation result, they are more likely to remember to do so. Researchers studied the impact of allowing teacher-sanctioned cheat sheets, and the results show that allowing these tools fosters in students the notion that practice helps internalize content and skills; in other words, "While doing it, I learn" (Soares, Leão, & Araujo, 2021). Removing the stress of remembering conventions on demand frees students to do it properly and focus on producing work that addresses the prompt (and frees you from answering questions about topics during your high concentration mode).

FINESSE FEEDBACK

Focusing feedback on the degree of success allows a more holistic approach to grading. For example, always consider the goal when providing feedback. Is the student reaching the benchmark included in the goal? If so, to what level? If falling short of the goal, how? What feedback could you provide to help the student refocus and reach the goal? Instead of assessing one final grade, provide feedback in stages and in focused areas to help the student move closer to the goal, with supports along the way. If the assignment has multiple drafts involved, grade specific aspects of each draft along the way. For example, I may check for thesis, topic sentences, and proper source citations on an outline, then move on to something more thematic, such as successfully building an argument or addressing the counterargument, for the final draft. Students can rest assured that the previously checked elements are in solid shape before submitting the final draft, lifting some of the pressure and anxiety that can accompany a big assessment.

This same approach can work well in subjects other than English language arts. Consider your classroom goal. Is there a way to break down the progression of student learning and their ability to demonstrate it in stages on a long-range assignment? For example, if a student in a vocal or instrumental music class can select a piece of music, the first stage of assessment is the selection's appropriateness. If a student selects a piece out of reach (in terms of difficulty level or out of vocal range), they are unlikely to succeed in the final assessment. After approving a selection, the next step may involve memorizing words or notes. Breaking down the assessment in the natural stages of learning will help students manage the larger tasks and increase the likelihood of a successful final product.

Working on Professional Advancement

If our work-life balance is out of whack, it's difficult to imagine taking on more work and stress, so the first items on the chopping block are usually those that we consider to be "extra." How can we consider adding a graduate class when we have a huge stack of papers to grade every night? How can we spend time writing a grant proposal when buried in planning and curriculum writing? How can we fit in homework from a professional development workshop?

However, there are types of pursuits that offer a high return on your investment. You may move up to a new salary band by taking additional coursework, for example. Many states offer educators loan forgiveness or stipends for National Board Certification. Finally, professional development boosts teacher self-efficacy, which can positively affect the following (Smet, 2022).

- Teachers' instructional practices
- Teachers' psychological well-being and job satisfaction (lessening the chance for burnout)
- Student motivation and achievement

Try writing a grant proposal. Prioritize asking for what you and your students need; it is time well spent. For example, I requested funds for five bicycling desk bikes. Now, some students have the option of pedaling during class to get the wiggles out while they work.

Finding grants may feel like an impossible task, but once you dig into it, you will find many opportunities to improve your classroom. You might start at the We Are Teachers website (www.weareteachers.com/education-grants). It includes a section directory for specific types of grants, such as STEAM, literacy, and arts. It also provides useful tips and guidelines for writing grant applications with practical advice. Search carefully for those that feel right for you and your classroom. Once you find a good fit, consider using generative AI to help you with portions of the application by using the actual grant description as a rubric for your application. Generative AI can help you see where you are meeting the criteria and where you may need to add more information.

Ask your district parent teacher organization if they have grants up for grabs, and check national websites such as the following.

- In Australia: GrantConnect (https://help.grants.gov.au)
- In Canada: Canada GrantWatch (https://canada.grantwatch.com/cat/42/teachers-grants.html)
- In the United States: USA Grant Applications (https://usagrantapplications.org)

The money is there for the taking (or the requesting).

Writing Letters of Recommendation

You might get what feels like an overwhelming number of requests to write letters of recommendation for college. Some schools and scholarship applications require the students to submit letters from their English teacher. That means *me*. It's my responsibility to find a way to carve out the time to help them. High concentration mode is the time to do it. Writing a letter with errors, the wrong pronoun, or scant details is not going to help the student. It may seem to be a tedious task, but it does require focus and concentration to produce your best work possible.

You can request a copy of the student's résumé or require them to complete a survey (like that in the reproducible "Letter of Recommendation Request Form," page 76) that asks for specific information and details that you might include in the letter. When you have this information, find a good boilerplate draft match. For example, I have boilerplate drafts saved with filenames that describe the students' roles, such as *class officer* or *newspaper editor*. Using a boilerplate template to begin writing a new letter for a student with a similar profile can prompt you to include specific types of details that relate to that profile. It also prompts you to add specific details such as community service and club activities (which are in the student's submitted form).

Of course, each boilerplate letter is just a springboard for customizing for the current student, but it is an excellent way to get started and save time.

Reflection Questions

Consider the following questions as you apply this information to your work.

- What can AI do for you in the classroom? Does an assignment need a better rubric? Is there a grant you would love to earn for your classroom?
- How can you generate more high concentration mode time for both you and your students? Is there a learning objective that would benefit from a group project that requires high concentration to produce?
- What do *you* want? If it's more personal time and work-life balance, how can you eliminate or revise some grading tasks to focus on what gets you closer to your goal?

Letter of Recommendation Request Form

Please return this form to me by:
Your name:
Notable courses and clubs:
Favorite academic experience from this class (The more specific you are, the more personal and interesting I can make your letter.):
Intended field or major of study in college (if you know):
Specific courses that you have taken already to prepare for that course of study:
Leadership roles and experiences:
Awards, jobs, experiences, activities, or services that make you unique from your peers. Think about anything you spend time on, even if it isn't something that is publicly acknowledged. (If these are on your résumé, you need not write them again.)
What, if anything, would you like this letter of recommendation to highlight about you?

EPILOGUE

No one enters this profession with the hope of exhaustion. Will there always be one more thing we could have done to make our classroom learning environment better? Of course, but at what cost? Modeling a healthy and balanced adult life begins with us in our classroom. Showing up every day with enthusiasm and motivation to help move students toward their goals will energize your classroom and make learning fun. Wisely using your time by selecting the tasks and activities that best fit the concentration modes that you and your students are in will result in dividends—with students, colleagues, friends, family, and yourself.

Using this technique positioned me to be the best colleague and teacher I could be. When another teacher took an unexpected leave of absence, I had the bandwidth to take on some of that person's duties.

Consider what you would do with an extra hour in your day. What about an extra fifteen minutes?

Would you run copies for a colleague? Join the committee that hosts social events for staff? Organize a common area for your department? There are so many ways to make a difference.

Take the reins.

The more you maximize your teacher time at work, the less it will encroach on your evenings and weekends. Your nights do not need to be the second shift of your teaching day. So, what are *your* goals? When was the last time you felt you had time to consider and mindfully plan for those? Also, this is true: The better *person* you are, the better *teacher* you will be.

Teacher time management is an art, and the more you practice matching the tasks to low, medium, and high modes, the more time you will have to create what else you need—including rest. Notice your mode and time: for your students, for yourself, and for your life. I wish you well in identifying your classroom modes and learning to maximize your teacher time.

REFERENCES AND RESOURCES

Allen, K., Gray, D. L., Baumeister, R. F., & Leary, M. R. (2022). The need to belong: A deep dive into the origins, implications, and future of a foundational construct. *Educational Psychology Review, 34*(2), 1133–1156.

Allen, K., Vella-Brodrick, D., & Waters, L. E. (2016). Fostering school belonging in secondary schools using a socio-ecological framework. *The Australian Educational and Developmental Psychologist, 33*(1), 1–25.

Bailey, K., & Jakicic, C. (2023). *Common formative assessment: A toolkit for Professional Learning Communities at Work* (2nd ed.). Solution Tree Press.

Bates, A. (2013). *The case against homework: Why it doesn't help students learn.* Accessed at https://resilienteducator.com/classroom-resources/the-homework-debate-the-case-against-homework on March 27, 2024.

Brookhart, S. M. (2017). *How to give effective feedback to your students* (2nd ed.). ASCD.

Calderón, M. E., & Slakk, S. (2018). *Teaching reading to English learners, grades 6–12: A framework for improving achievement in the content areas.* Corwin.

Center for Teaching Innovation. (n.d.). *Peer assessment.* Accessed at https://teaching.cornell.edu/teaching-resources/assessment-evaluation/peer-assessment on September 11, 2024.

Cervantez, D. J., & Gutierrez, A. S. (2019). *Stories from the field: Fostering positive peer relationships.* Accessed at https://files.eric.ed.gov/fulltext/ED601208.pdf on September 12, 2024.

Cohn, J. (2021). *How to prepare for the next phase of hybrid teaching.* Accessed at www.chronicle.com/article/how-to-prepare-for-the-next-phase-of-hybrid-teaching on September 12, 2024.

Cooper, A. Z., & Richards, J. B. (2016). Lectures for adult learners: Breaking old habits in graduate medical education. *Alliance for Academic Internal Medicine, 130*(3), 376–381.

Couros, G. (Host). (2021, May 30). Capturing the Classroom: A convo with Ellen Linnihan episode [Video podcast episode]. In *The innovator's mindset podcast.* Accessed at www.youtube.com/watch?v=kHqw5IS-3Vc on December 30, 2024.

Cox, J. (2019). *Dealing with cleanliness in the classroom.* Accessed at www.thoughtco.com/dealing-with-cleanliness-in-the-classroom-2081581 on September 12, 2024.

Csapai, E. G., Varga, D., & Berke, S. (2020). Analysis of time management and self-management work practice by leaders—a focus group study. *Applied Studies in Agribusiness and Commerce, 14*(3–4), 133–140.

Cui, Y., Schunn, C. D., Gai, X., Jiang, Y., & Wang, Z. (2021). Effects of trained peer vs. teacher feedback on EFL students' writing performance, self-efficacy, and internalization of motivation. *Frontiers in Psychology, 24*(12), 788474. doi: 10.3389/fpsyg.2021.788474

Davidson, N., Major, C., & Michaelsen, L. (Eds.). (2014). Small-group learning in higher education: Cooperative, collaborative, problem-based, and team-based learning. *Journal on Excellence in College Teaching, 25*(4).

de Bono, E. (1995). *Tactics: The art and science of success.* Gardners Books.

DeLussey, S. (n.d.). *How to cope with teaching stress* [Blog post]. Accessed at www.mrsdscorner.com/how-to-cope-with-teaching-stress on November 19, 2024.

Dikker, S., Haegens, S., Bevilacqua, D., Davidesco, I., Wan, L., Kaggen, L., et al. (2020). *Morning brain: Real-world neural evidence that high school class times matter.* Accessed at www.ncbi.nlm.nih.gov/pmc/articles/PMC7745151 on March 28, 2024.

Education Support. (n.d.). *Time management: A guide for teachers and education staff.* Accessed at www.educationsupport.org.uk/resources/for-individuals/guides/time-management-and-wellbeing-at-work on September 12, 2024.

Eli Review. (n.d.). *Giving helpful feedback in Eli Review.* Accessed at https://elireview.com/learn/tutorials/students/giving-helpful-feedback on September 11, 2024.

Ennis, R. P., Royer, D. J., Lane, K. L., & Dunlap, K. D. (2020). Behavior-specific praise in pre-K–12 settings: Mapping the 50-year knowledge base. *Behavioral Disorders, 45*(3), 131–147. https://doi.org/10.1177/0198742919843075

Ericsson, K. A. (2006). The influence of experience and deliberate practice on the development of superior expert performance. In K. A. Ericsson, N. Charness, P. J. Feltovich, & R. R. Hoffman (Eds.), *The Cambridge handbook of expertise and expert performance* (pp. 683–703). Cambridge University Press. https://doi.org/10.1017/CBO9780511816796.038

European Commission. (2023). *How can artificial intelligence assist teachers with formative and summative assessment?* Accessed at https://school-education.ec.europa.eu/en/discover/news/how-can-artificial-intelligence-assist-assessment on September 12, 2024.

Facing Our History and Ourselves. (2020). *Socratic seminar.* Accessed at www.facinghistory.org/resource-library/socratic-seminar on March 29, 2024.

Fancourt, A. (2018). *Listen and respond: Evaluating the use of audio feedback.* Accessed at https://my.chartered.college/impact_article/listen-and-respond-evaluating-the-use-of-audio-feedback on September 12, 2024.

Ferlazzo, L. (2021). *What are the best strategies for small-group instruction?* Accessed at www.edweek.org/teaching-learning/opinion-what-are-the-best-strategies-for-small-group-instruction/2021/11 on September 11, 2024.

Francis, J. (2022, August 17). *5 benefits of small group instruction w/ lesson plan examples* [Blog post]. Accessed at https://blog.alludolearning.com/benefits-of-small-group-instruction on October 27, 2024.

Frydenberg, E. (2011). The utility of coping: What we have learned and how we can develop skills during adolescence. In T. J. Devonport (Ed.), *Managing stress: From theory to application* (pp. 201–228). Nova Science Publishers.

Gallup. (2019). *Creativity in learning.* Accessed at www.gallup.com/education/267449/creativity-learning-transformative-technology-gallup-report-2019.aspx on September 11, 2024.

Gamber-Thompson, L. (2019). *How sustained silent reading keeps students curious and engaged.* Accessed at www.edsurge.com/news/2019-10-07-how-sustained-silent-reading-keeps-students-curious-and-engaged on September 11, 2024.

Gazith, K. (2024). *The power of effective reading instruction: How neuroscience informs instruction across all grades and disciplines.* Solution Tree Press.

GBAO. (2022). *Poll results: Stress and burnout pose threat of educator shortages.* Accessed at www.nea.org/sites/default/files/2022-02/NEA%20Member%20COVID-19%20Survey%20Summary.pdf on March 27, 2024.

Gehringer, E. F. (2017). *Helping students to provide effective peer feedback.* Accessed at https://peer.asee.org/helping-students-to-provide-effective-peer-feedback.pdf on September 11, 2024.

Goddard, R. (2023, May 6). *Making feedback more effective for your students* [Blog post]. Accessed at https://blog.irisconnect.com/uk/community/blog/making-feedback-more-effective-for-your-students on September 12, 2024.

Goldratt, E. M., & Cox, J. (2012). *The goal: A process of ongoing improvement (40th anniversary ed.).* North River Press.

Gonser, S. (2020). *6 smart ways to bring the power of music into your classroom.* Accessed at www.edutopia.org/article/6-smart-ways-bring-power-music-your-classroom on September 12, 2024.

Good, T. L., & Brophy, J. E. (2003). *Looking in classrooms* (9th ed.). Allyn & Bacon.

Gray, D. L. , Hope, E. C., & Matthews, J. S. (2018). Black and belonging at school: A case for interpersonal, instructional, and institutional opportunity structures. *Educational Psychologist, 53*(2), 97–113. doi: 10.1080/00461520.2017.1421466

Hamilton, I. (2023). *Artificial intelligence in education: Teachers' opinions on AI in the classroom.* Accessed at www.forbes.com/advisor/education/it-and-tech/artificial-intelligence-in-school on March 25, 2024.

Happy Healthy Teacher. (2022). *How to leave work at work when you're a teacher.* Accessed at https://healthyhappyteacher.com/how-to-leave-work-at-work-teacher on August 21, 2024.

Harvard Kennedy School. (n.d.). *Using small groups to engage students and deepen learning in new HKS classrooms, study notes of computer networks.* Accessed at www.hks.harvard.edu/sites/default/files/Academic%20Dean's%20Office/Guide%20to%20Small-Group%20Learning.pdf on August 9, 2024.

Hasbrouck, J. (2006). *For students who are not yet fluent, silent reading is not the best use of classroom time.* Accessed at www.aft.org/ae/summer2006/hasbrouck on September 12, 2024.

Hattie, J., & Timperley, H. (2007). The power of feedback. *Review of Educational Research, 77*(1), 81–112.

Hawe, E., Dixon, H., & Hamilton, R. (2021). Why and how educators use exemplars. *Journal of University Teaching and Learning Practice, 18*(3). https://doi.org/10.53761/1.18.3.10

References and Resources

Hemmingson, E. (2019, October 3). *5 reasons to incorporate more downtime in your school day* [Blog post]. Accessed at https://teacherwellnesscenter.com/blog/teacher-downtime on September 12, 2024.

Hopfenbeck, T., Zhang, Z., Sun, S. Z., Robertson, P., & McGrane, J. (2023). Challenges and opportunities for classroom-based formative assessment and AI: A perspective article. *Frontiers in Education, 8*. doi:10.3389/feduc.2023.1270700.

Hopkins, G. (2007, October 15). *"Sustained silent reading" helps develop independent readers (and writers)*. Accessed at www.educationworld.com/a_curr/curr038.shtml on September 10, 2024.

Hough, L. (2023). *The problem with grading*. Accessed at www.gse.harvard.edu/ideas/ed-magazine/23/05/problem-grading on September 10, 2024.

Huang, W. (2023, August 23). *Using formative AI for assignments*. Accessed at https://fltmag.com/formative-ai on March 27, 2024.

HundrED. (2017). *Cleaning tradition*. Accessed at https://hundred.org/en/innovations/cleaning-tradition on December 2, 2024.

Ice, P., Curtis, R., Phillips, P., & Wells, J. (2007). Using asynchronous audio feedback to enhance teaching presence and students' sense of community. *Journal of Asynchronous Learning Networks, 11*(2), 3–25.

Jabr, F. (2013). *Why your brain needs more downtime*. Accessed at www.scientificamerican.com/article/mental-downtime on September 12, 2024.

Jackman, C. (2024, February 20). *The 3 R's for teacher self-care: Reflect. Release. Recharge.* [Blog post]. Accessed at www.pbs.org/education/blog/the-3-rs-for-teacher-self-care-reflect-release-recharge on August 21, 2024.

Jorgenson, J. (2023). *5 research-based reasons to use brain breaks in the classroom and brain break resources*. Accessed at www.jeremyajorgensen.com/5-research-based-reasons-to-use-brain-breaks-in-the-classroom-and-brain-break-resources on September 10, 2024.

Jung, J. Y., Tyack, L., & von Davier, M. (2022). Automated scoring of constructed-response items using artificial neural networks in international large-scale assessment. *Psychological Test and Assessment Modeling, 64*(4), 471–494.

Juvonen, J., Espinoza, G., & Knifsend, C. (2012). The role of peer relationships in student academic and extracurricular engagement. In S. L. Christenson, A. L. Reschly, & C. Wylie (Eds.), *Handbook of research on student engagement* (pp. 387–401). Springer Science + Business Media. https://doi.org/10.1007/978-1-4614-2018-7_18

Kalmbach, D. A., Schneider, L. D., Cheung, J., Bertrand, S. J., Kariharan, T., Pack, A. I., et al. (2017). Genetic basis of chronotype in humans: Insights from three landmark GWAS. *Sleep, 40*(2), zsw048. doi: 10.1093/sleep/zsw048

Kappa Delta Pi. (2022, January 13). *4 steps to student-friendly learning targets* [Blog post]. Accessed at www.kdp.org/blogs/community-manager/2022/01/13/4-steps-to-student-friendly-learning-targets on October 27, 2024.

Kelly, M. (2020). *The importance of organization for teachers.* Accessed at www.thoughtco.com/teachers-as-organizers-8339 on March 28, 2024.

Killingback, C., Drury, D., Mahato, P., & Williams, J. (2020). Student feedback delivery modes: A qualitative study of student and lecturer views. *Nurse Education Today, 84,* 104237. doi: 10.1016/j.nedt.2019.104237

Kirwin, A., Raftery, S., & Gormley, C. (2023). Sounds good to me: A qualitative study to explore the use of audio to potentiate the student feedback experience. *Journal of Professional Nursing, 47,* 25–30.

Klein, A. (2020). *There are smart ways to use time to aid learning. Why do so many schools ignore them?* Accessed at www.edweek.org/leadership/there-are-smart-ways-to-use-time-to-aid-learning-research-shows-why-do-so-many-schools-ignore-them/2020/02 on September 11, 2024.

Larson, K. (2022, March 1). *Can the classroom environment make teachers more (or less) effective*? [Blog post]. Accessed at https://ideas.demco.com/blog/classroom-environment-and-teacher-effectiveness on March 31, 2024.

Linnihan, E. (2022). *Capturing the classroom: Creating videos to reach students anytime.* Solution Tree Press.

Liu, O. L., Rios, J. A., Heilman, M., Gerard, L., & Linn, M. C. (2016). *Validation of automated scoring of science assessments.* Accessed at www.frontiersin.org/journals/education/articles/10.3389/feduc.2023.1270700/full on September 12, 2024.

Lyubykh, Z., & Gulseren, D. B. (2023). *How to take better breaks at work, according to research.* Accessed at https://hbr.org/2023/05/how-to-take-better-breaks-at-work-according-to-research on August 9, 2024.

Markman, T. (2023). *Using AI for writing? Prompt it properly.* Accessed at www.linkedin.com/pulse/using-ai-writing-prompt-properly-tiffany-markman on September 12, 2024.

Mautner, R. (2022). *The "Vivaldi effect": Three centuries later.* Accessed at https://ideamagazine.com/the-vivaldi-effect-three-centuries-later on September 11, 2024.

References and Resources

McCombs, B. (2015). *Developing responsible and autonomous learners: A key to motivating students.* Accessed at www.apa.org/education-career/k12/learners on September 11, 2024.

McDonald, J. (n.d.). *Tuning protocol.* Accessed at https://schoolreforminitiative.org/doc/tuning.pdf on March 27, 2024.

Midwest Comprehensive Center at American Institutes for Research. (2018). *Student goal setting: An evidence-based practice.* Accessed at https://files.eric.ed.gov/fulltext/ED589978.pdf on March 27, 2024.

Millis, B. J. (2014). Using cooperative structures to promote deep learning. *Journal on Excellence in College Teaching, 25*(3&4), 139–148.

Mind Help. (2023). *Listening to classical music improves memory, study finds.* Accessed at https://mind.help/news/classical-music-improves-memory-vivaldi-effect on August 21, 2024.

Minshew, A. (2023, November 10). *What is teacher self-care and how do you practice it?* [Blog post]. Accessed at www.waterford.org/education/teacher-self-care-activities on August 21, 2024.

Mol, S. E., & Bus, A. G. (2011). To read or not to read: A meta-analysis of print exposure from infancy to early adulthood. *Psychological Bulletin, 137*(2), 267–296.

Moshman, R. (n.d.). *I stopped taking work home, and it's made me a better teacher and parent.* Accessed at www.boredteachers.com/post/i-stopped-taking-work-home on October 27, 2024.

National Center on Safe Supportive Learning Environments. (n.d.). *Relationships.* Accessed at https://safesupportivelearning.ed.gov/topic-research/engagement/relationships on September 12, 2024.

National Education Association. (2019). *How much homework is too much?* Accessed at www.nea.org/professional-excellence/student-engagement/tools-tips/how-much-homework-too-much on September 12, 2024.

Ness, M. (2024). *Read alouds for all learners: A comprehensive plan for every subject, every day, grades preK–8.* Solution Tree Press.

Núñez, J. L., & León, J. (2015). Autonomy support in the classroom: A review from self-determination theory. *European Psychologist, 20*(4), 275–283. https://doi.org/10.1027/1016-9040/a000234

Okada, R. (2021). Effects of perceived autonomy support on academic achievement and motivation among higher education students: A meta-analysis. *Japanese Psychological Research, 65*(3), 230–242.

OpenAI. (2024). *ChatGPT* (June 16 version) [Large language model]. https://chat.openai.com/chat

Ortlieb, E., & Cheek, E. H., Jr. (Eds.). (2013). *School-based interventions for struggling readers, K–8.* Emerald Group Publishing.

Osterman, K. F. (2023). Students' need for belonging in the school community. *Review of Educational Research, 70*(3), 323–367.

Ozan, C., & Kincal, R. Y. (2018). The effects of formative assessment on academic achievement, attitudes toward the lesson, and self-regulation skills. *Educational Sciences: Theory and Practice, 18*(1), 85–118.

Parrish, C. (2022). *Teachers face mental health crisis because of low pay, pandemic stress, scant support.* Accessed at https://azmirror.com/2022/07/29/teachers-face-mental-health-crisis-because-of-low-pay-pandemic-stress-scant-support on October 7, 2024.

Paul, A. M. (2016, August 2). *Researchers find that frequent tests can boost learning.* Accessed at www.scientificamerican.com/article/researchers-find-that-frequent-tests-can-boost-learning on March 29, 2024.

Penney, C. (2024). *8 reasons why one on one teaching benefits students* [Blog post]. Accessed at www.proxlearn.com/blog/8-reasons-why-one-on-one-teaching-benefits-students on August 21, 2024.

Pepler, D., & Bierman, K. L. (2018). *With a little help from my friends: The importance of peer relationships for social-emotional development.* Accessed at https://prevention.psu.edu/wp-content/uploads/2022/05/rwjf450248-PeerRelationships-1.pdf on September 12, 2024.

ReDesign. (2021). *Key personalized learning practices: Conferences and feedback.* Accessed at www.redesignu.org/wp-content/uploads/2021/03/Instruction_-Conferencing-Feedback_reDesign.pdf on August 21, 2024.

Ripiceanu, R. (2023). *A complete guide to flexible teaching.* Accessed at https://spark.school/a-complete-guide-to-flexible-teaching on September 12, 2024.

Roosevelt, F. D. (1933). *First inaugural address.* Accessed at www.gilderlehrman.org/sites/default/files/inline-pdfs/First%20Inaugural%20Address.pdf on December 30, 2024.

Rowe, D. A., Mazzotti, V. L., Ingram, A., & Lee, S. (2017). Effects of goal-setting instruction on academic engagement for students at risk. *Career Development and Transition for Exceptional Individuals, 40*(1), 25–35.

Rundle, M. (2012). *Five predictions sci-fi author Ray Bradbury got right.* Accessed at www.huffingtonpost.co.uk/2012/06/06/ray-bradbury-dead-how-accurate-predictions-fahrenheit-451_n_1574126.html on March 27, 2024.

References and Resources

Schiel, J., Bobek, B. L., & Schnieders, J. Z. (2023). *High school students' use and impressions of AI tools.* Accessed at www.act.org/content/dam/act/secured/documents/High-School-Students-Use-and-Impressions-of-AI-Tools-Accessible.pdf on March 31, 2024.

Scott, T. (Director). (1986). *Top Gun.* Paramount Pictures.

Serna, F. (2021). *Key lessons: What research says about the value of homework.* Accessed at https://latam.cengage.com/key-lessons-what-research-says-about-the-value-of-homework on September 12, 2024.

Sharma, H. L., & Saarsar, P. (2017). PMI (plus-minus-interesting): A creative thinking strategy to foster critical thinking. *International Journal of Academic Research and Development, 2*(6), 974–977.

Sides, J. D., & Cuevas, J. (2020). Effect of goal setting for motivation, self-efficacy, and performance in elementary mathematics. *International Journal of Instruction, 13*(4), 1–16.

Slinkman, A. (2023, March 27). *A simple tool for peer feedback in the Art Room.* Accessed at https://theartofeducation.edu/2016/04/peer-feedback-helping-students-glow-grow on March 26, 2024.

Smet, M. (2022). Professional development and teacher job satisfaction: Evidence from a multilevel model. *Mathematics, 10*(1), 1–17.

Soares, F., Leão, C. P., & Araujo, S. (2021). *Cheat sheets and Padlet: A metacognitive learning tool.* Accessed at https://dl.acm.org/doi/abs/10.1145/3434780.3436677 on March 27, 2024.

Staake, J. (2023, July 22). *20 ways teachers can use CHATGPT to make their lives easier.* Accessed at www.weareteachers.com/chatgpt-for-teachers on March 27, 2024.

Stuart, D. (2020). *How (and why) to leave audio feedback on student work this year, whether during in-person or distance learning.* Accessed at https://davestuartjr.com/how-and-why-to-leave-audio-feedback-on-student-work-distance-learning on August 10, 2024.

Tom, T. (2023). *The jigsaw method teaching strategy.* Accessed at www.teachhub.com/teaching-strategies/2016/10/the-jigsaw-method-teaching-strategy on August 21, 2024.

Touchstone Research. (2023). *Generative AI through the eyes of Gen Z* [Infographic]. Accessed at https://touchstoneresearch.com/generative-ai-through-the-eyes-of-gen-z-infographic on March 31, 2024.

Tutt, P. (2021). *Teaching kids to give and receive quality peer feedback.* Accessed at www.edutopia.org/article/teaching-kids-give-and-receive-quality-peer-feedback on August 21, 2024.

Tuzunkan, E. (2023). *How to use journaling to improve time management.* Accessed at https://healthyofficehabits.com/how-to-use-journaling-to-improve-time-management on March 28, 2024.

Umejima, K., Ibaraki, T., Yamazaki, T., & Sakai, K. L. (2021). *Paper notebooks vs. mobile devices: brain activation differences during memory retrieval.* Accessed at www.frontiersin.org/journals/behavioral-neuroscience/articles/10.3389/fnbeh.2021.634158/full on September 12, 2024.

Vittorini, P., Menini, S., & Tonelli, S. (2021). An AI-based system for formative and summative assessment in data science courses. *International Journal of Artificial Intelligence in Education, 31*(2), 159–185.

Wahlen, A., Kuhn, C., Zlatkin-Troitschanskaia, O., Gold, C., Zesch, T., & Horbach, A. (2020). Automated scoring of teachers' pedagogical content knowledge—a comparison between human and machine scoring. *Frontiers in Education, 149.* https://doi.org/10.3389/feduc.2020.00149

Walker, T. (2022). *Survey: Alarming number of educators may soon leave the profession.* Accessed at www.nea.org/nea-today/all-news-articles/survey-alarming-number-educators-may-soon-leave-profession on September 12, 2024.

Wallace, K. (2015). *Kids have three times too much homework, study finds; what's the cost?* Accessed at www.cnn.com/2015/08/12/health/homework-elementary-school-study on September 12, 2024.

We Are Teachers. (2024, March 6). *45 best education grants for teachers and schools.* Accessed at www.weareteachers.com/education-grants on March 27, 2024.

Weimer, M. (2018). *The benefits of study groups.* Accessed at www.facultyfocus.com/articles/course-design-ideas/what-students-can-learn-from-studying-together on September 10, 2024.

Western University Centre for Teaching and Learning. (n.d.). *Grading strategies.* Accessed at https://teaching.uwo.ca/teaching/assessing/grading-strategies.html on March 31, 2024.

Wiklund-Hörnqvist, C., Jonsson, B., & Nyberg, L. (2014). Strengthening concept learning by repeated testing. *Scandinavian Journal of Psychology, 55*(1), 10–16.

Winters-Robinson, E. (2019). *We asked teachers what they'd do with ten extra minutes a day. Here's what they said.* Accessed at www.edsurge.com/news/2019-09-30-we-asked-teachers-what-they-d-do-with-ten-extra-minutes-a-day-here-s-what-they-said on August 21, 2024.

Writing Across the Curriculum Clearinghouse. (n.d.). *How can I get the most out of peer review?* Accessed at https://wac.colostate.edu/repository/teaching/intro/peer on March 27, 2024.

Yee, K. (n.d.). *Grading student writing: Tips and tricks to save you time.* Accessed at www.usf.edu/atle/documents/handout-grading-writing-assignments.pdf on August 8, 2024.

Yibing, L., Lynch, A. D., Kalvin, Liu, J., & Lerner, R. M. (2011). Peer relationships as a context for the development of school engagement during early adolescence. *International Journal of Behavior Development, 35*(4), 329–342.

INDEX

A

academic vocabulary, 59
agendas, 38, 39
artificial intelligence (AI)
    creating assessments and, 65–66
    feedback and, 72
    grading assessments and, 69–70
    identifying the goal and, 8, 9
    school policies and, 66
assessments
    adjusting, 70–72
    artificial intelligence and, 65–66, 69–70
    common formative assessments, 63, 64
    creating assessments, 63–69
    grading assessments, 69–73
    low concentration mode and, 28, 32–33
    resources, tapping into online, 64–65
    rubrics and, 66–69
    streamlining and, 11–12
    test preparation, 31, 32–33
attention span, 52

B

Bradbury, R., 65
breaks, 35, 52
building community for social-emotional activities, 38
burnout, impact of, 2

C

chronotypes, 62
collaboration, 63
common formative assessments, 63, 64. *See also* assessments
communication

drafting emails for future send and medium concentration mode, 52–53
sending communications and low concentration mode, 40
working from home and, 63
community, building community for social-emotional activities, 38
conferencing, 13–15

D

discussions or reviews, whole-class, 46
diurnal preferences, 62
downtime, 28

E

emails, drafting for future, 52–53
exemplars and letting students in on the goal, 10
extensions, instructions for, 46

F

feedback
    artificial intelligence and, 72
    assessments and, 33, 72–73
    group-recorded feedback, 18–19
    peer-guided feedback, 15–17
    streamlining and, 12
    verbal feedback, 28, 51
    voice memo feedback, 18
flexibility and flexible teaching, 20–21, 29
formative one-to-one conferencing, 13–15

G

goals
    about, 7–8
    determining where you can streamline, 10–12
    flexible teaching and being fluid, 20–21
    identifying the goal, 8–9
    letting students in on, 9–10
    reflection questions, 21
    reproducibles for, 22–26
    streamlining the process, 13–20
Goddard, R., 51
grading
    creating a key for, 69
    electronic grading tools, 70
    grading assessments, 69–73
    grading brief writings, 50, 53
    proficiency-based grading, 33
    streamlining and, 11–12
    working from home and, 63
grant writing, 73–74
group-recorded feedback, 18–19
Gruetzmacher, B., 58

H

high concentration mode. *See also* modes of concentration
    about, 3, 57–58
    planning for, 53–54
    reflection questions, 75
    reproducibles for, 76
    student activities for, 58–61
    teacher activities for, 61–75
    time and, 62
homework, 12, 19–20
housekeeping, 41–42
Huang, W., 66

I

I can statements, 10
incentives and rewards, 60
instructions

Index

focusing more time on and grading assessments, 72
instructional or tutorial videos, 46–47
interviews, three-step interviews, 48
introduction
    about this book, 5
    modes of concentration, 2–3
    why this book, 3–4

J

jigsaw, 48, 49

L

lectures, 46
letters of recommendation, 74–75, 76
low concentration mode.
    See also modes of concentration
    about, 3, 27–28
    benefits of, 29
    reflection questions, 42
    streamlining and, 11
    student activities for, 28–34
    teacher activities for, 34–42
    time and, 37

M

matching the mode philosophy, 50
medium concentration mode.
    See also modes of concentration
    about, 3, 43–44
    reflection questions, 54
    reproducibles for, 55
    student activities for, 44–50
    teacher activities for, 50–54
    time and, 45, 51
modes of concentration.
    See also specific modes of concentration
    about, 2–3

matching the mode philosophy, 50
mode shifting, 11
multimodal learning, 41
music, use of, 41

O

one-to-one conferencing, 13–15
organization
    example folder setup, 37
    organizing digital content, 36
    organizing tangible items, 35–36

P

partner work, 31–32
peer-guided feedback, 15–17
planning
    collaboration and, 63
    lesson planning time, 57
    medium concentration mode and, 50, 51, 53–54
    working from home and, 63
plus, minus, interesting (strategy), 59, 60, 61
podcasts, 60–61
pro-con-caveat grids, 48
professional advancement and professional development, 73–74
projects, creating, 61

R

reading
    read-alouds, 60–61
    self-guided reading or writing, 44
    sustained silent reading (SSR), 59
redos, 33
relationships
    low concentration mode and, 29
    one-to-one conferencing and, 13

small-group learning and, 50
voice memo feedback and, 18
reproducibles for
 college planning sheet, 22
 daily log, 55
 letter of recommendation request form, 76
 peer analysis form, 26
 peer edit rubric—argument research paper, 24–25
 preconference form, 23
rubrics, 16, 66–69

S

self-care, 35, 38
self-guided reading or writing, 44
sentence starters, 16
slide shows and low concentration mode, 34
small groups
 impact of, 49–50
 low concentration mode and, 31–32
 medium concentration mode and, 45, 48–50
 verbal feedback for small groups or one-to-one, 51
social-emotional activities, building community for, 38
Socratic seminars, 71
standards and identifying goals, 9
streamlining. *See also* goals
 determining where you can streamline, 10–12
 streamlining the process, 13–20
sustained silent reading (SSR), 59

T

test preparation, 31, 32–33
Theory of Constraints, 4

think-pair-share, 48
three-step interviews, 48
throbbing bag syndrome, 11
time logs, 43, 55
Top Gun (1986), 58
turn-and-talk, 48
tutorials, 10, 39, 44, 45, 47

V

videos
 creating projects, 61
 educational and entertaining videos, 44
 instructional or tutorial videos, 44–45, 45–48
 permission for, 48
 upsides of, 46
 watching or responding to read-alouds, videos, or podcasts, 60–61
vocabulary, academic vocabulary, 59

W

whole-class discussions or reviews, 46
wiggle breaks, 35
working in small groups and with partners, 31–32. *See also* partner work; small groups
writing
 grading brief writings, 53
 grant writing, 73–74
 letters of recommendation, 74–75, 76
 peer-guided feedback and, 15–16
 self-guided reading or writing, 44
 student-led small-group work and, 49

Y

your goal and streamlining. *See* goals

Capturing the Classroom
Ellen I. Linnihan
Harness the power of video to cultivate equity, create stability, and reach students anytime. With *Capturing the Classroom*, you will learn concrete and doable ways to record lectures, classroom discussions, tutorials, review sessions, and more to support any content area or curriculum.
BKF998

You're a Teacher Now! What's Next?
Tom Hierck and Alex Kajitani
Trusted education experts Tom Hierck and Alex Kajitani draw from their experiences to offer research-backed tools and strategies in an easily referenced FAQ format that both new and veteran teachers can use in their classrooms to address everything from behavior management to self-care planning.
BKG142

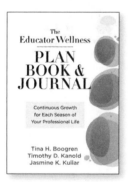

The Educator Wellness Plan Book and Journal
Tina H. Boogren, Timothy D. Kanold, and Jasmine K. Kullar
This plan book and journal serves as a companion guide to *Educator Wellness: A Guide for Sustaining Physical, Mental, Emotional, and Social Well-Being*. Prioritize four dimensions of wellness with weekly routines and reflection prompts to help you commit to wellness practices throughout the school year.
BKG139

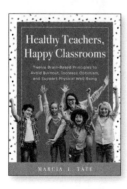

Healthy Teachers, Happy Classrooms
Marcia L. Tate
Best-selling author Marcia L. Tate delivers 12 principles proven by brain research to help you thrive personally and professionally. Each chapter digs into the benefits of these self-care strategies and offers suggestions for bringing the practice to life in your classroom.
BKG044

Solution Tree | Press

Visit SolutionTree.com or call 800.733.6786 to order.

GL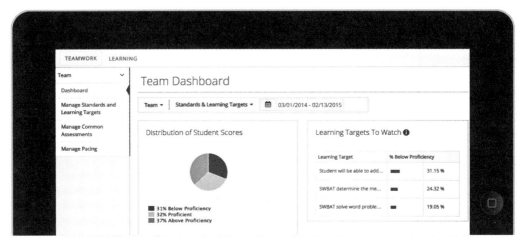BAL PD

The **Power to Improve**
Is in Your Hands

Global PD gives educators focused and goals-oriented training from top experts. You can rely on this innovative online tool to improve instruction in every classroom.

- Get unlimited, on-demand access to guided video and book content from top Solution Tree authors.
- Improve practices with personalized virtual coaching from PLC-certified trainers.
- Customize learning based on skill level and time commitments.

▶ **REQUEST A FREE DEMO TODAY**
SolutionTree.com/GlobalPD